高职高专
国际商务应用
系列教材

外贸业务口语

（第2版）

龙 芸 张芷楣 主编

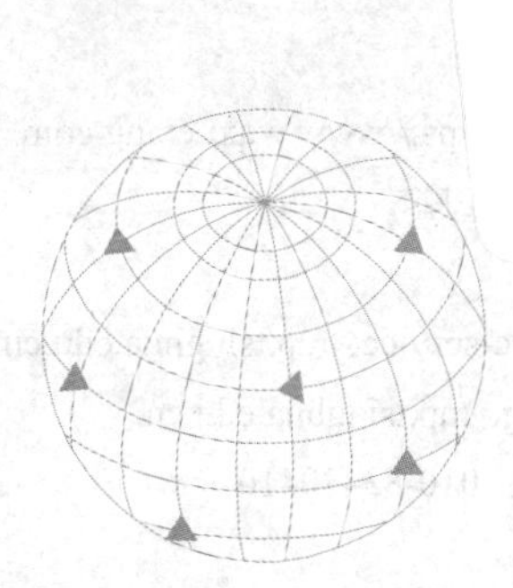

清華大学出版社
北 京

内 容 简 介

本书共12个单元，第1~4单元主要从机场接待、餐厅接待、酒店接待、工厂参观四个方面阐述如何做好接待服务，给客户留下良好的印象；第5~11单元主要从产品介绍、价格谈判、付款方式、装运、包装、保险、签订合同七个方面探讨如何在外贸谈判中取得双赢；第12单元介绍如何处理客户索赔。同时，本书配备丰富的在线课程、微课、课件等教学资源，扫描书中二维码即可观看学习。

本书所配套的在线课程"外贸业务口语"在2021年被评为广东省高等职业教育精品在线开放课程，在2023年入选广东省高等职业院校课程思政示范计划立项名单。

本书可作为国际经济与贸易、国际商务、商务英语、跨境电子商务、外贸英语等相关专业的教材，同时也可作为广大英语及外贸爱好者的自学教材。

图书在版编目（CIP）数据

外贸业务口语 / 龙芸，张芷楣主编. — 2版. — 北京：清华大学出版社，2024.4
高职高专国际商务应用系列教材
ISBN 978-7-302-65725-5

Ⅰ.①外… Ⅱ.①龙… ②张… Ⅲ.①对外贸易－英语－口语－高等职业教育－教材 Ⅳ.①F75

中国国家版本馆CIP数据核字（2024）第051313号

责任编辑：聂军来
封面设计：傅瑞学
责任校对：刘　静
责任印制：刘海龙

出版发行：清华大学出版社
　网　　址：https://www.tup.com.cn, https://www.wqxuetang.com
　地　　址：北京清华大学学研大厦A座　　**邮　　编**：100084
　社 总 机：010-83470000　　**邮　　购**：010-62786544
　投稿与读者服务：010-62776969，c-service@tup.tsinghua.edu.cn
　质量反馈：010-62772015，zhiliang@tup.tsinghua.edu.cn
　课件下载：https://www.tup.com.cn，010-83470410
印 装 者：三河市铭诚印务有限公司
经　　销：全国新华书店
开　　本：185mm×260mm　　**印　　张**：10.25　　**字　　数**：189千字
版　　次：2020年9月第1版　2024年5月第2版　　**印　　次**：2024年5月第1次印刷
定　　价：39.00元

产品编号：103331-01

本书编委会

主　编　龙　芸　张芷楣

编　委　何紫云　梁　匡

第2版前言

随着全球经济一体化的深入推进、“一带一路”倡议的不断扩展和《区域全面经济伙伴关系协定》(RCEP)的实施，中国与外国在经济、文化等领域的相互联系与合作日益紧密，培养复合型国际化人才已经成为国内外高等院校的普遍共识。英语作为国际通用语言，在对外贸易领域中具有重要地位，外贸英语受到越来越多高等院校的关注。

“外贸业务口语”是外贸英语专业的核心课程，它不仅融合了谈判沟通技巧，而且更加大了谈判中口语训练的强度和力度，重点突破学生羞于表达、无法表达和表达不清的困境，帮助学生提高口语技能，让学生能更加顺畅地进行外贸谈判。本书深入贯彻党的二十大精神，坚持立德树人的理念，书中内容为培养学生在外贸商务谈判过程中的口语交际技能，学习与项目主题相关的中国优秀传统文化、贸易强国发展举措、商务社交礼仪、职场道德规范等，培养学生树立文化自信和崇高理想，具有爱国情怀和国际视野，在外贸商务谈判中展示大国风采，成为合格的社会主义建设者和接班人。本书适合外贸英语专业和国际贸易专业教学选用，充分体现了培养国际化外贸专业人才的特色。

本书所配套的在线课程“外贸业务口语”在2021年被评为广东省高等职业教育精品在线开放课程，在2023年入选广东省高等职业院校课程思政示范计划立项名单。

本书是以外贸公司的一笔业务档案为蓝本，设计了工作过程及各个项目。整个工作流程共设12个项目，即12个单元，包括机场接待、餐厅接待、酒店接待、工厂参观、产品介绍、价格谈判、付款方式、装运、包装、保险、签订合同和索赔。每个单元均以外贸业务员与外贸跟单员岗位中典型工作项目为主线，统筹考虑前后课程内容。教材内容来源于职业岗位、课程标准和党的二十大精神中外贸行业发展内容，以工作过程先后顺序化课程内容，把整个教学过程和课程思政教育贯穿于一种实际的工作过程中，对学生进行潜移默化、润物细无声的教育，形成育人有高度、教育有温度的专业教材。

本书的每一个单元设计逻辑清晰、从易到难、层层递进，方便教师教学和学生学习。每一单元分别由Warm-up Activities（热身活动）、Vocabulary（生词 & 词组）、Model Dialogues（经典对话）、Practice（练一练）、Knowledge Zone（知识拓展）五部分组成。

Warm-up Activities由3个任务组成，即图片描述、讨论和小组演示。学生先通过第一个任务中的图片获取跟本单元学习相关的词汇及表达，再通过第二个任务中的讨论掌握一些必要的背景知识，最后通过第三个任务中的演示操练本单元的重点学习内容。这3个任务循序渐进的口语热身活动为接下来的对话实战做了良好的准备，活跃了课堂气氛。

Vocabulary把本单元出现的所有生词和词组都罗列了出来，并配上音标，有助于学生认读和理解即将学习的对话。

Model Dialogues精选了2个跟单元主题相关的经典对话，对话内容不仅囊括外贸业务的重点和难点，还展示享有国际盛名的中国制造、中国品牌和中国企业等，把爱国主义情怀贯穿于学习中。在每个对话的后面，还附加了不同场景下的句型，丰富了学生的语言表达。

Practice包含3个任务，即连线题、翻译题和创意角色扮演。连线题重点考查学生的情景对话能力；翻译题重点考查学生的口语表达能力；颇具特色的创意角色扮演任务赋予不同学生不同的任务要点，促使他们思维碰撞、呈现精彩纷呈的对话，有利于学生之间互相取长补短，共同进步。

Knowledge Zone结合党的二十大精神，介绍与单元主题相关的中国优秀传统文化、贸易强国发展举措、商务社交礼仪、职场道德规范等，用社会主义核心价值观铸魂育人，在推进课程思政过程中为学生打造一个自我延伸的知识角，帮助学生坚定文化自信、树立崇高理想，具有爱国情怀和国际视野。

本书由龙芸、张芷楣担任主编，负责全书的策划、选材、统稿与整合。具体分工如下:龙芸负责第3、4、7、8、10、12单元，张芷楣负责第1、2、5、6、9、11单元。同时，感谢资深企业专家何紫云和梁匡在本书编写过程中给予了宝贵的指导意见并协助了审稿。

为了方便教师教学和学生学习，本书配有详尽的教学课件、微课、在线课程和题库等。

由于本书编者水平有限，书中难免存在不足和疏漏之处，恳请专家和读者批评指正。

编　者

2023年12月

第1版前言

本书不仅融合了谈判沟通技巧，更加大了谈判口语训练的强度和力度，重点突破学生羞于表达、无法表达和表达不清的问题，帮助学生提高口语技能，让学生能够更加顺畅地进行外贸谈判。本书适合外贸英语和国际贸易等相关专业使用，充分体现了培养国际化外贸专业人才的特色。

本书是以外贸公司的一项业务档案为蓝本，设计了工作流程和各个项目。整个工作流程共设12个项目，即12个单元，包括机场接待、餐厅接待、酒店接待、工厂参观、产品介绍、价格谈判、付款方式、装运、包装、保险、合同签订和索赔。每个单元均以外贸业务员与外贸跟单员岗位中的典型工作项目为主线，统筹考虑前后课程内容。本书内容来源于职业岗位和课程标准，根据企业发展需要和完成岗位工作所需要的知识、能力、素质，参照人力资源和社会保障部的相关标准，按工作流程的先后顺序编写，把整个教学过程贯穿于实际工作流程之中，突出职业技能、职业道德、职业素养的培养，为学生的可持续发展奠定良好基础。

本书不仅关注外贸谈判工作的全过程，而且注重培养学生在外贸商务接待过程中处理问题的能力和职业岗位综合能力。本书内容与实际职业活动实现最大限度地“无缝对接”，从而激发学生主动学习的兴趣，达到提高交际能力的目的。因此，本书每个教学单元的设计逻辑清晰、从易到难、层层递进，便于教师教学和学生学习。每个单元分别由Warm-up Activities、Vocabulary、Model Dialogues、Practice及Knowledge Zone五部分组成。

Warm-up Activities部分由三个任务组成，即图片描述、讨论和小组演示。学生先通过第一个任务中的图片获取与本单元相关的词汇及表达，再通过第二个任务中的讨论掌握一些必要的背景知识，最后通过第三个任务中的演示操练本单元的重点学习内容。这三步循序渐进的口语热身活动既为接下来的对话实战做了良好的铺垫，也能起到活跃课堂气氛的作用。

Vocabulary部分把本单元出现的重点单词和词组挑选出来，并配上音标，有助于学生识读和理解即将学习的对话内容。

Model Dialogues部分精选了两个与单元主题相关的对话，体现外贸业务的重点和难点，非常具有代表性。在每个对话的后面，还附加了不同场景下的常用句型，用来丰富学生的语言表达。

Practice部分包含三个任务，即匹配题、翻译题和创意角色扮演。匹配题重点考查学生的情景对话能力；翻译题重点考查学生的口语表达能力；颇具特色的创意角色扮演任务赋予学生不同的任务要点，促使他们碰撞思维、呈现精彩纷呈的对话，有利于学生之间互相取长补短、共同进步。

Knowledge Zone部分为学生打造了一个自我延伸的知识角，作为课堂学习的有益补充，有利于拓宽学生的视野，加深对外贸业务口语学习的认知。

本书由龙芸、张芷楣负责全书的策划、选材、统稿与整合。具体分工如下：龙芸负责第3、4、7、8、10、12单元；张芷楣负责第1、2、5、6、9、11单元。同时感谢企业专家何紫云和梁匡在本书编写过程中给予了宝贵的指导意见并协助审稿。为方便教师教学和学生学习，本书配有丰富的教学课件、微课等资源。

由于编者水平有限，书中难免存在疏漏和不足，恳请读者批评指正。

编　者

2020年3月

目 录

Unit 1
At the Airport

Learning Objectives

- Introduce yourself to a new customer.
- Etiquette of exchanging business cards.
- Talk about the flight/trip.
- Say airport farewell and wishes to the customer.
- Master expressions of welcoming guests.

Warm-up Activities

Task 1

◆ Brainstorming:

Look at the following pictures and express them in English.

Task 2

◆ Discussion:

If you are at the airport to meet foreign guests, how do you check the flight information of your guests?

Task 3

◆ Presentation:

Choose one topic from below and present it to the class.

(1) What should be prepared in advance to welcome guests at the airport?

(2) What etiquette should we bear in mind to welcome guests at the airport?

Vocabulary

import ['ɪmpɔːt] *n.* 进口
export ['ekspɔːt] *n.* 出口
pleasure ['pleʒə(r)] *n.* 愉快，满足
airline ['eəlaɪn] *n.* 航空公司
straight [streɪt] *adv.* 笔直地，直接
crew [kruː] *n.* 全体乘务人员
customs ['kʌstəmz] *n.* 海关
emergent [i'mɜːdʒənt] *adj.* 紧急的
fruitful ['fruːtfl] *adj.* 富有成效的
expansion [ɪk'spænʃn] *n.* 扩张，扩展
frequently ['friːkwəntli] *adv.* 频繁地，经常地
business card ['bɪznəs kɑːd] 名片
sales manager ['seɪlz 'mænɪdʒə(r)] 销售经理
information desk [ˌɪnfə'meɪʃn desk] 问询处

Model Dialogues

Dialogue 1

(Lu Fei, a sales manager of Guangzhou Foreign Trade Import & Export Company, is welcoming his new customer John Smith from America.)

Lu: Excuse me, are you Mr. Smith from America?

John: Yes, I am.

Lu: It's a great pleasure to meet you[1], Mr. Smith. I'm Lu Fei, a sales manager of Guangzhou Foreign Trade Import & Export Company. This is my business card.

John: This is mine. How do you do, Mr. Lu? (Shaking hands)

Lu: How do you do, Mr. Smith? (Shaking hands)

John: It's very kind of you to come and meet me at the airport.

Lu: My pleasure. How was your flight? [2]

John: Oh, it was long but quite comfortable. The airline I was flying provided excellent services.

Lu: Did you have any trouble clearing customs?

John: No, it was quick and efficient. The staff of China are nice.

Lu: Welcome to Guangzhou, Mr. Smith.

John: Thank you. I have heard a lot about Guangzhou before.[3] It's modern and beautiful.

Lu: I hope you can enjoy your stay here. You must be tired after the long flight. Can I take you straight to the hotel and take some rest?

John: Sure. I feel a bit tired. I think it's the jet lag[4].

Lu: Let me help you with your luggage, Mr. Smith.

John: Thank you. I can manage it.[5]

Notes:

[1] It's a great pleasure to meet you. 很高兴能见到你。

本句还可以表达为 Nice to meet you. /Glad to meet you. /It's good to meet you. 在日常接待中，常常会用到单词 pleasure, 要注意不同短语的区别。如：

—Thanks for your help.（感谢你的帮助。）

—My pleasure.（不客气。）

此外，面对别人致谢时，还可以用 With pleasure. /Don't mention it. /You are welcome. / Not at all. /Any time. 如：

—Could you pass me the salt, please?（请把盐递给我，好吗？）

—With pleasure.（很乐意。）

[2] How was your flight?（你的飞行旅途如何？）询问客人旅途情况时可以使用。

[3] I have heard a lot about Guangzhou before. 我久闻广州这座城市的大名了。

[4] jet lag 时差反应

[5] I can manage it. 我能搞定。

More to Learn for Dialogue 1

1. Asking about the trip

(1) How was the trip/flight/journey?

(2) Did you have a pleasant journey?

(3) Did everything go all right during the trip?

2. Talking about the trip

(1) I was held up for a few hours at Shanghai Hongqiao International Airport because of a small accident.

(2) It was very comfortable, except for a little bit of turbulence.

(3) It was great. The airline I was flying provided excellent services.

(4) Long, but quite comfortable. ABC Airline treats its passengers well.

Dialogue 2

(David, a sales assistant of Xinhua Foreign Trade Import & Export Company, is seeing off a client named Johnson on behalf of his superior, Mr. Gao.)

David: Mr. Johnson, we are so sorry that we haven't done too much to show you around these days. I'm here to see you off on behalf of my manager[1], Mr. Gao. He was eager to come but was tied up by[2] some emergent issues this morning.

Johnson: Thank you so much, David. It's very kind of you to see me off. (Shaking hands) Please say thanks for me to Mr. Gao, too.

David: I will. I hope you can stay longer next time to visit some tourist attractions in Guangzhou, such as Canton Tower and Baiyun Mountain.

Johnson: Sure. I've had a wonderful time here. I'm glad to return to Mexico with good memories and fruitful business outcomes.

David: I feel the same way. By the way, your visit helps to promote the friendship and understanding between us.

Johnson: I'm glad you think so. I believe, with the expansion of business, we'll contact more frequently in the future. I hope you'll visit us someday in Mexico.

David: That would be wonderful. Thank you!

Johnson: I guess it's time for me to say goodbye.

David: Have a safe journey back.[3] Goodbye.

Johnson: Thanks!

Notes:

[1] on behalf of sb 代表某人

[2] be tied up by sth 受到……的阻碍

[3] Have a safe journey back. 一路平安！

More to Learn for Dialogue 2

1. Seeing Off Customers

(1) Time flies!

(2) How I wish you could stay here a little bit longer!

(3) It's a pity that you have to leave so soon.

(4) It's been a great pleasure to have you with us.

(5) I guess it's time for us to say goodbye.

(6) Please remember me to your CEO.

(7) We hope you'll visit us again.

2. Wishes to Customers

(1) Have a good trip!

(2) Goodbye, take care!

(3) Wish you a safe landing!

(4) Have a safe flight!

Practice

Practice One: Matching

Match the sentences in the left column with the correct responses in the right column. Each sentence has only one response.

A. I had a long flight but I'm doing well. It is very kind of you to meet me at the airport, Mr. Wilson.	1. That would be best. I really need to take some rest.
B. May I help you with your luggage?	2. Yes. I'd like to see some historic spots such as the Summer Palace and the Temple of Heaven.
C. You must be tired after such a long flight. Can I take you straight to your hotel?	3. I appreciate that, but I'd rather spend a quiet evening in the hotel getting ready for tomorrow's meeting.
D. How long did the flight take?	4. No. It was fast and efficient.
E. Is this your first trip to Guangzhou?	5. It's my pleasure. Let's get you to your hotel so you can get some rest.
F. Are there any sights you'd like to see while you are in Beijing?	6. More than twelve hours, including the transfer time.
G. How about having an informal dinner with us tonight?	7. Yes. I've visited China several times, but it's my first visit to Guangzhou.
H. Did you have any trouble clearing customs?	8. No, thanks. I can manage it.

A. __________ B. __________ C. __________ D. __________

E. __________ F. __________ G. __________ H. __________

Practice Two: Blank Filling

Fill in each blank in English based on the Chinese meaning.

(1) David: Did you have a good trip?

Johnson: Yes, ____.

（除了有点颠簸，飞行还是挺舒服的。）

(2) Let me ____.

（让我来帮您拿行李吧。）

(3) He is ____________________ and sends ____________________.

（他非常想见您，让我先代他向您问好。）

(4) Have you been ____?

（有没有人把您介绍给我们的新总裁？）

(5) We're sorry that ____.

（很抱歉，您在中国时我们对您帮助很不够。）

(6) I must ____.

（我必须要向您和在场的诸位告别了。）

Situational Practice: Creative Tasks

(1) You are Hu Jie, a sales manager of Zhejiang ABC Import & Export Corporation. You are welcoming Susan White from Mexico at the airport. It is the first time for you to meet each other. Make a dialogue and you should:

- hold a pick-up sign and exchange business cards,
- ask about the trip,
- assist with the luggage.

(2) You are Chen Fang, the general manager of BNT Trading Company. You are seeing off Sally Jones, the general manager of a New York company. During Sally's visit in China, you took her to some famous tourist attractions in Guangzhou. Make a dialogue and you should:

- give a positive comment on Sally's visit,
- express the desire to cooperate further,
- say wishes to Sally's trip/flight.

(3) Suppose you are at the airport to welcome an important client. Ask about the client's opinion and confirm details of his schedule. Remember to include meeting arrangements, tourist attractions, food preference and other possible arrangements.

Knowledge Zone

I. Top Nine Tips on Business Card Etiquette

Here are nine basic rules to follow for the exchange of business cards.

(1) Take plenty of cards with you. There is nothing more unprofessional than a business person to say "Oh, I'm sorry. I just gave out my last card." or " I'm sorry. I didn't bring any with me."

(2) Keep your cards in a business card case or in something that protects them from wear and tear. A crumpled business card makes a poor first impression.

(3) Know where your business cards are at all times. The person who has to go through every jacket and pants pocket or every nook and cranny of a briefcase to find his business cards loses credibility immediately.

(4) Hand them out with discretion.

(5) Give and receive cards with your right hand — the hand of discretion. This can make a big difference when doing business internationally.

(6) Give the card with the client's familiar language side up so the person who is receiving it can read it without having to turn it around.

(7) Always make a comment about a card when you receive it. Note the logo, the business name or some other pieces of information.

(8) Keep your business cards up to date. When any of your contact information changes, run, don't walk, to your nearest printer for new cards.

(9) Don't write notes to yourself on someone else's business card during the exchange unless they appear relevant.

II. How to Pick Someone Up from the Airport?

- To avoid a long wait, plan to arrive at the airport about 30 minutes after someone's flight is scheduled to land.
- Wait until your party is outside to meet them at the curb (most airports prohibit parking more than 5~10 minutes at the curb outside of terminals).
- Schedule a taxi or rideshare car to pick up your party if you can't make it. If they're over 25 years old, consider booking them a rental car.

Method 1 Finding out Flight Details and Timing Your Arrival

1. Know which airline your party will arrive on.

Most airports have multiple terminals, with different airlines flying out of each. If you know which airline your traveler is flying with, then you know the general area of the airport that you need to be in to meet them.

- Look for the signs for their airline. For example, if your traveler is flying with Delta Airlines, look for the Delta Airline signs at the terminal.
- Check the airport's website to find what terminal the airline your traveler is flying with uses.

2. Check the status of their flight before you leave for the airport.

Make sure you have your traveler's flight number so you can check the status of their flight before you actually head out. If their flight is delayed, canceled, or redirected, it will affect when you need to leave.

- Go to the airline's website or the airport's website to check the status of the flight. Look for the airline and flight number.
- Call the airport to ask for the flight status.

3. Find out if they have any checked bags.

It can take a fair amount of time for checked bags to make their way from the airplane to the baggage carousel. Parking your vehicle at the curb outside of the terminal is prohibited, so make sure your traveler has picked up their bags and is ready for you to pick them up before you pull up to the curb.

- If your party is coming back from an international trip, they will likely have a checked bag. They may also have brought things back with them that require them to go through customs, which can take longer for them to make their way through the airport.

4. Arrive 30 minutes after their flight is scheduled to land.

If you try to time your arrival for when your traveler's plane lands then you could be waiting a long time before they actually make it out of the terminal. It takes a while to get off the plane, pick up any baggage they may have, and make their way through the airport. Time your arrival to be about half an hour after they're set to land so you don't have to wait around for them.

Tip: International flights may require your party to go through customs and can take longer for them to get their luggage. Plan on arriving 45 minutes to an hour after their flight is scheduled to land.

Method 2 Meeting the Traveler at the Airport

1. Have your traveler call you when they land.

An easy way to know when you should pull up to the curb or make your way to the concourse to meet them is to have your traveler call you when they're getting off the plane. Planes can sometimes be stuck on the tarmac, so having your traveler call you can keep you up to date on their whereabouts.

They can also tell you exactly where they want you to meet them so you can get in and out quickly.

2. Park your car in the short-term parking lot if you plan to meet them.

If you have to travel a great distance to pick up your party from the airport, plan on parking at the airport and waiting inside for them to arrive. Flights can be unpredictable and you don't want to end up arriving too late or too early without being able to wait comfortably in the terminal.

- Park in the airport's short-term parking lots to save on costs.
- If you're traveling from a distance, parking in the short-term lot can allow you to relax and wait in the airport for your party to arrive.

3. Meet your traveler outside of their terminal if you're not picking them up curbside.

If you do decide to park and wait for your party inside the airport, wait in the area outside of their terminal for their airline. Going through airport security to meet them at their arrival gate can be time-consuming and may be prohibited.

- Many airports have restaurants and cafes outside of the security check that you can use to kill some time before your party arrives, but you can't wait for several hours or they may ask you to leave to make room for customers and travelers.
- Even if your party doesn't have any checked bags, the baggage claim areas are often near the exits, so they're still a convenient place to meet.

4. Avoid parking if you're picking up curbside.

If you're simply picking up your party from the curb outside of the terminal, parking is time-consuming and an unnecessary cost. Instead, arrange for your traveler to meet you at the curb.

- If you arrive too early, drive off-site or wait somewhere nearby for your traveler to land and make their way through the terminal. Parking at the curb is prohibited at most airports.

5. Wait until your party is outside to meet them at the curb.

It's prohibited at most airports to wait more than 5~10 minutes at the curb outside of the terminals. In order to follow the airport's rules and to be courteous to other people picking up their parties, wait until your traveler is actually standing at the curb with their bags before you drive around to pick them up.

- Have your traveler call you when they're heading to the curb with their bags.
- If you can't contact your traveler, keep circling around their terminal until you see them standing outside.
- International arrivals may take longer to make their way through the airport because they have to go through customs.

Guidance on Tails of Airline Companies

Unit 2
At the Restaurant

Learning Objectives

- Invite guests to dinner.
- Ask about food preferences.
- Order food and drinks.
- Talk about food and drinks.
- Propose a toast to business outcomes.

Warm-up Activities

Task 1

◆ Brainstorming:

Look at the following pictures and express them in English.

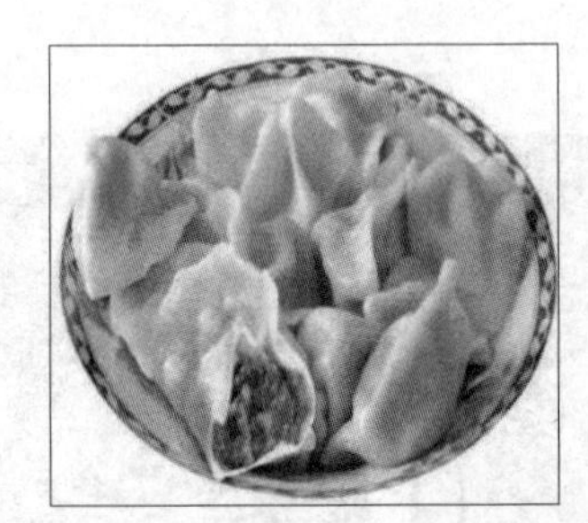

Task 2

◆ Discussion:

If you are going to have dinner with a foreign customer, what should you take into consideration before you book a restaurant table/order food?

Task 3

◆ Group Presentation:

Choose three famous dishes from Cantonese cuisine and introduce them to your class. Focus on cuisine and ingredients.

Vocabulary

recommendation [ˌrekəmen'deɪʃn]	*n.* 推荐
specialty ['speʃəlti]	*n.* 特色菜
filling ['fɪlɪŋ]	*n.* 馅料
clam [klæm]	*n.* 蛤蜊
shrimp [ʃrɪmp]	*n.* 虾
leek [liːk]	*n.* 韭葱
must-have [mʌst hæv]	*n.* 必备品
vegetarian [ˌvedʒə'teəriən]	*n.* 素食者；*adj.* 素食者的
dessert [dɪ'zɜːt]	*n.* 甜品
keen [kiːn]	*adj.* 热衷于，喜爱
custard ['kʌstəd]	*n.* 奶冻，蛋挞
spicy ['spaɪsi]	*adj.* 辣的
lettuce ['letɪs]	*n.* 生菜，莴苣
aperitif [əˌperə'tiːf]	*n.*（饭前）开胃酒
stir-fried spinach [stɜː(r) fraɪd 'spɪnɪtʃ]	炒菠菜
deep-fried tofu [diːp fraɪd 'təʊfuː]	炸豆腐
dry martini [draɪ mɑː'tiːni]	干马丁尼
dry sherry [draɪ 'ʃeri]	干雪莉酒
Chef's Special [ʃɛfs 'speʃl]	主厨特餐
green pepper [ˌgriːn 'pepə(r)]	青椒
T-bone steak [ˌtiː bəʊn 'steɪk]	丁骨牛排
black pepper sauce [blæk 'pepə(r) sɔːs]	黑椒汁
garden salad [ˌgɑːdn 'sæləd]	田园沙拉
cream soup [kriːm suːp]	（奶油）浓汤
Thousand Island dressing ['θaʊznd 'aɪlənd 'dresɪŋ]	千岛酱
French onion soup [frentʃ 'ʌnjən suːp]	法式洋葱汤
walnut brownie ['wɔːlnʌt 'braʊni]	核桃巧克力蛋糕

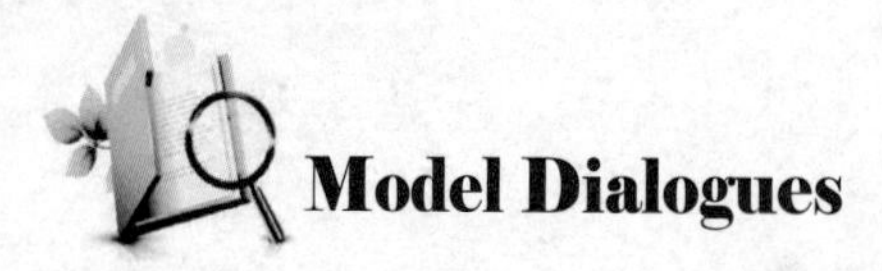

Model Dialogues

Dialogue 1

(Lin Xue and Zhang Feng are having dinner with their British customers, Tyler and Lisa, at a local Chinese restaurant in Foshan.)

(Ordering food.)

Lin: We hope that you can enjoy the food here. It's some of the best in the city.

Tyler: Well, thanks for inviting. There is a great number of dishes on the menu.

Lin: Tyler, are there any types of food you don't like?

Tyler: No, everything is OK. Do you have any recommendations?

Zhang: The home-style lettuce wrap[1] is the restaurant's specialty. The filling is cooked with clams, shrimps, green pepper and leeks. It is one of the famous dishes from Cantonese Cuisine.

Lin: I strongly recommend the steamed freshwater fish[2]. People pay special attention to heating time when they steam the fish in order to create a tender taste. It is almost a must-have for local family dinners.

Lisa: Wow, the food culture here is impressive. By the way, are there any dishes for vegetarians?

Lin: Sure, we can get some stir-fried spinach and an order of deep-fried tofu.

Lisa: That's great.

Tyler: And I see there are some local desserts on the menu.

Lin: We could order some double-layer milk custard[3] if you like.

Tyler: Why not? I'm always keen to try the local food.

Zhang: I don't want to put you on the spot[4], but may I ask if you are comfortable using chopsticks?

Lisa: We've used chopsticks before, but maybe you could help us ask for some forks, just to be safe.

(During dinner.)

Zhang: How do you like the spicy chicken?

Tyler: It is fantastic. And the steamed fish is fresh and tasty.

Lin: Does anyone want another bowl of rice?

Lisa: Not right now, but thanks for asking.

Zhang: Tyler and Lisa, thank you again for visiting us here in Shunde. I'd like to make a toast [5] to our continued cooperation and mutual benefits it brings.

Zhang, Lin, Tyler, Lisa: Cheers!

Notes:

[1] home-style lettuce wrap 家常生菜卷

[2] steamed freshwater fish 可以翻译为"清蒸淡水鱼"。鲫鱼是crucian carp，草鱼是grass carp，鲤鱼是carp，鳗鱼是eel。

[3] double-layer milk custard 双皮奶，源于顺德大良的一种传统甜品。

[4] put sb on the spot 让某人难堪、尴尬

[5] make a toast 举杯，通常用于提议祝酒的时候。提议祝酒时可以用I'd like to make a toast/propose a toast to our continued cooperation.（我提议为我们持续合作举杯！）祝酒时可以说Cheers（干杯），一饮而尽时可以说Bottoms up（干杯）。

More to Learn for Dialogue 1

1. Inviting guests to dinner

(1) I wonder if you have any plans tonight.

(2) I wonder if you are doing anything special tonight.

(3) May I invite you to dinner?

(4) Shall we have dinner together?

(5) Would you like to have dinner with me?

2. Accepting the dinner invitation

(1) I'd be delighted to go.

(2) Yes, I'm glad to come.

(3) Not yet for the moment. /Not really.（当别人询问是否有安排时）

3. Rejecting the dinner invitation

(1) I'm afraid I won't be available this afternoon.

(2) Let me check my schedule. I'm sorry that I have a lunch meeting tomorrow.

(3) I'd love to, but I have a busy schedule these days.

Dialogue 2

(Kevin Tang, a sales manager of Guangming Manufacturing Company, is in a western restaurant with Shirley, his new client from Australia.)

Waiter: Good evening, madam and sir. Do you have a reservation?

Kevin: Yes, we've reserved a window view table for two. And the table is reserved under the name of Kevin Tang.

Waiter: Welcome to our restaurant, Mr. Tang. This way, please.

Kevin: Thank you.

Waiter: Please take your seats. Here is the drink menu. Shall I bring you some aperitif ?

Kevin: I'll have a dry martini with soda. What about you, Shirley?

Shirley: A medium dry sherry, please.

Waiter: One dry Martini with soda, and one medium dry sherry. Shall I take your order now?

Shirley: We are still browsing. Do you have any recommendations?

Waiter: What about the Chef's Special today, our award-winning T-bone steak? [1] I suggest you try this.

Shirley: That's a good idea. We'll have the T-bone steak with black pepper sauce.

Waiter: How would you like your steak done?

Shirley: Medium well[2] with mashed potatoes, please. What about you, Kevin?

Kevin: I want it medium rare, with mushrooms and carrots. Also, one house salad with Thousand Island dressing[3] and cream soup.

Shirley: I will have French fries and pickles as sides, one Cesar salad and French onion soup.

Waiter: All right. Any desserts?

Shirley: One walnut brownie, please.

Kevin: Make it two.

Waiter: (Repeats the order) Dear sir and madam, the food will be served soon.

Notes:

[1] What about the Chef's Special today, our award-winning T-bone steak? 要不试下我们今天的主厨特餐，我们的获奖菜品丁骨牛排?

[2] medium well 表示“七分熟”。其他表示牛排熟度的表达分别有 rare（一分熟）、medium rare（三分熟）、medium（五分熟）、medium well（七分熟）以及 well done（全熟）。

[3] Thousand Island dressing 表示“千岛酱”。沙拉所配的酱料一般称为 salad dressing 而不是 salad sauce。

More to Learn for Dialogue 2

1. Asking about dining preferences

(1) Which do you prefer, brandy or red wine?

(2) Are you keen on seafood?

(3) Are you a vegetarian?

(4) Do you have any food allergies?

2. Talking about dining preferences

(1) I don't care much about spicy food.

(2) I am allergic to nuts and dairy products.

(3) I prefer vanilla syrup to chocolate syrup.

Practice

Practice One: Matching

Match the sentences in the left column with the correct responses in the right column. Each sentence has only one response.

A. Do you like Chinese food?	1. Well, the onion soup is very good here. And the pepper steak is also wonderful.
B. What about eating out tonight?	2. No, it's my treat this time.
C. Would you like a drink while you look at the menu?	3. Sure. It's marvelous, and I think it's the best in the world.
D. Could you recommend something special here?	4. Yes, of course. Maotai wine is the best Chinese wine. It would be a pity if you left without tasting it.
E. Let's go Dutch as usual, David.	5. Yes, thank you. I'll have a Scotch on the rocks.
F. I've heard Maotai wine is very popular in China. Could we try some?	6. I'm afraid I can't. Shall we make it tomorrow?
G. What about some of this spicy cabbage?	7. Chopsticks will do. I'm learning to use them.
H. Do you want a knife and fork or chopsticks?	8. No, thanks. It's nice, but I don't care much for spicy food.

A. ________ B. ________ C. ________ D. ________

E. ________ F. ________ G. ________ H. ________

Practice Two: Blank Filling

Fill in each blanks in English based on the Chinese meaning.

(1) Mr. Smith, here is ____________________ this evening.

（史密斯先生，这儿有一封请柬，邀请您参加今晚在长城饭店举行的宴会。）

(2) China is ____.

（中国是一个拥有绝佳饮食文化的国家。）

(3) I suggest we start with ____________________, then ____________________.

（我建议我们先来盘杂拌凉菜开胃，然后是青豆虾仁、红烧海参。）

(4) Are you ______________________________?

（您可以点菜了吗？）

(5) Then let's ______________________________?

（那么我们就点糖醋鱼，好不好？）

(6) Here comes ____________________. Please ____________________, Mr. Ford.

（北京烤鸭来了。福特先生，请您自便。）

Situational Practice: Creative Tasks

(1) Helen is inviting her guest, Mr.Wells, an Australian business representative, to try the local specialties in Guangzhou. During the dinner, Helen is going to introduce Cantonese cuisine and some famous dishes. The conversation should include the following points:

- invite the guest to dinner,
- ask about food preference,
- ask if the guest is comfortable using chopsticks,
- introduce two famous dishes from Cantonese cuisine.

(2) Angela, a sales representative, is having dinner with Mr. Cornell in a western restaurant. Before the meal, they order some wine, steak, and salad. Make a conversation and include the following points:

- order drinks (or aperitifs),
- order steaks at their desired doneness,
- order salad with dressing.

(3) You are Fang Qing, a sales manager of ANC Manufacturing Co., Ltd. You are going to have dinner with a British client Karen Smith. Karen is a vegetarian. You are supposed to choose a proper restaurant, order in the restaurant and talk about Chinese food culture.

Knowledge Zone

I. Chinese Table Manners

A multitude of etiquette considerations occur when you are dining in China. Compared with western countries, there are some special differences in table manners in China.

(1) A round dining table is more popular than a rectangular or square one, as many people who can be seated comfortably around it conveniently face one another. The guest of honor is always seated to the right of the host; the next in line will sit on his left. Guests should be seated after the host's invitation, and it is discourteous to seat guests at the place where the dishes are served.

(2) Dining may only begin once the host and all his guests are seated. The host should actively take care of all his guests, inviting them to enjoy their meal.

(3) On a typical Chinese dining table there are always a cup, a bowl on a small dish, together with the chopsticks and spoons. Dishes are always presented in the center of the table.

(4) Apart from soup, all dishes should be eaten with chopsticks. There are many no-no's such as twiddling with chopsticks, licking chopsticks, or using them to stir up the food, gesture with them or point at others with them. Never stick chopsticks in the center of rice, as this is the way to sacrifice and is therefore considered to be inauspicious.

(5) Keep your dining pace accorded with other people. Never smoke when dining.

(6) A formal dining is always accompanied by tea, beer or distilled spirits. The one who sit closest to the teapot or wine bottle should pour them for others from the senior and superior to the junior and inferior. And when other people fill your cup or glass, you should express your thanks. Guests cannot pour tea or wine themselves.

(7) A toast to others is a characteristic Chinese dining. When all people are seated and all cups are filled, the host should toast others first, together with some simple prologue to let the dining start. After the senior's toast, you can toast anyone from superior to inferior at their convenience. When someone toasts you, you should immediately stop eating to drink and toast him or her in response. If you are far from someone you want to toast, then you can use your cup or glass to rap on the table to attract attention rather than raise your voice. However, it is impolite to urge others to drink.

(8) Conventionally, if you are invited to a formal banquet, all the dishes should not be eaten up completely, or you will give the host the impression that he has not provided a good banquet and the food was insufficient. After dining, guests should leave once the host has left the table.

II. Chinese Food Culture

1. Types of Courses

A Chinese meal is consisted of two parts: staple food, normally made of rice, noodles or steamed buns, vegetable and meat dishes. (It is different from Western meals, which take meat or animal protein as main dish). The primary eating utensils are chopsticks (for solid foods) and ceramic spoon (for soups and congees). In a Chinese meal, everyone will have their own rice bowl; however, the accompanying dishes will be served in communal plates and shared by all people. Normally, the dishes are often eaten together with a mouthful of rice. Desserts are not main course in China; instead, Chinese desserts are considered as snacks eaten between two meals. If dessert is served in the meal, they will be served during the course of meal with no firm distinction made. If served at the end of the meal, the dessert is normally fresh fruit.

2. Cold Dishes

Cold dishes are the first course in traditional Chinese banquet. Salt, sugar, chili powder, light soy sauce, vinegar and sesame oil are often used to make cold dishes. Cold dishes attach great importance to the designing of the dish, which is the "shape" of the dish. Normally, cold dish can provoke people's appetite.

3. Hot Dishes

Hot dish is a concept compared with cold dish. Normally, main course is also called hot dish. Hot dishes are normally cooked using techniques like stir-frying, deep-frying, Liu, quick-frying, Hui, etc.

4. Soups and Congees

Instead of adding milk or cream into the soup, refined starches from corn are added to chinese soups to thicken the soups. There are also light soups which don't use starches. Normal ingredients for soups are vegetables and meat like pork and chicken. Soups are served following hot dishes. Chinese people believe that soups are good for health.

Congee is a kind of porridge or gruel. Except for rice and other cereals, meat, fish and sometimes vegetables and flavorings are added into the congee. Congee is a good choice for breakfast. Congee is easy to digest, so it's a great choice for ill people and young infants.

5. Staple Food

Rice is the staple food in southern China, for southern China is the rice farming areas.

People always eat steamed rice. In contrast, in northern China, which is the wheat cultivation area, people normally eat flour-based food, like noodles, steamed buns and dumplings.

6. Features

As the famous French sinologist Jacques Gernet has stated, "There is no doubt that in this sphere China has shown greater inventiveness than any other civilizations." Indeed, Chinese are among the peoples of the world who have been particularly preoccupied with food and eating. This food culture has formed since the ancient time and is deeply rooted in traditional Chinese culture, including Yin-Yang and Five Elements, Confucianism, Traditional Chinese Medicine, cultural and artistic achievements and national characters.

7. Varied Flavors

China has a vast territory and abundant resources, and each region has different climate, natural products and folk customs. After a long time, different regions have formed their own food flavors. For example, people in southern China take rice as staple food, while people from northern China are used to eating noodles or steamed buns as staple food. As for the flavor, the whole country can be generally divided into four parts: sweet south, salt north, sour east and spicy west.

8. Different dishes in different seasons

Chinese people will change their menus as the switch of each season, from the raw materials to the cooking methods, each season uses different seasonings and accompany dishes. Winter has a thicker and rich flavor, while summer features in light and cool flavor; cuisines in winter are most braised or stewed, while in summer, they are mostly served as cold and dressed with sauces.

9. Aesthetic sense

Chinese cuisine puts great importance on the aesthetic sense of the dish, and pursues the harmony in color, aroma, taste, shape and utensil. The aesthetic sense of the cuisine can be expressed from multiple aspects. No matter the raw material is Chinese cabbage or carrot, they can all be cut into different shapes to match the whole dish, which gives people a highly unified mental and physical enjoyment.

Guidance to Utensils in a Formal Western Dinner

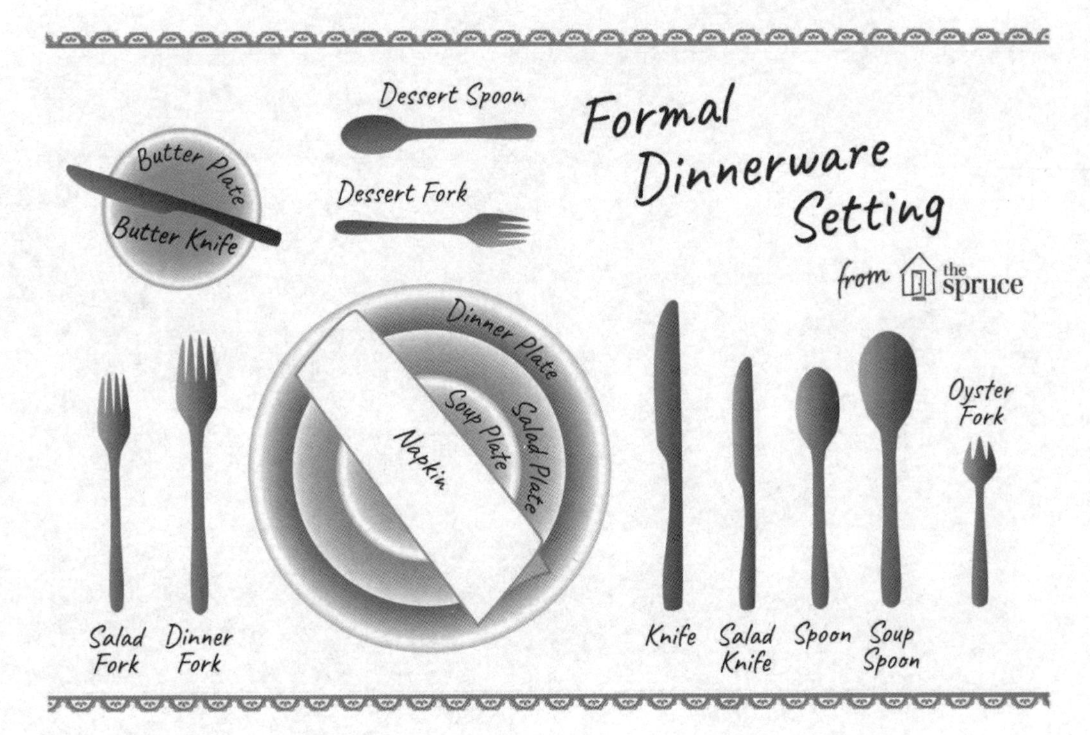

Unit 3
At the Hotel

Learning Objectives

- Know how to check in.
- Ask about room services.
- Handle problems with accommodation.
- Know how to check out.
- Master the basic expressions about check-in and check-out.

Warm-up Activities

Task 1

◆ Brainstorming:

Look at the pictures below, and think about what should be prepared for your accommodation in a hotel.

Task 2

◆ Discussion:

Suppose you are going to take a business trip to New York. How do you book a room in a hotel?

Which way of booking a room is your favorite, and why?

Task 3

◆ Group Presentation:

When you are at the hotel, what information would you like to know from hotel receptionists? Think it over and present it to the class.

Vocabulary

reservation [ˌrezəˈveɪʃn] *n.* 预订
bellboy [ˈbelbɔɪ] *n.*（旅馆的）行李员
extend [ɪkˈstend] *v.* 延长，扩大
recreation [ˌrekriˈeɪʃn] *n.* 娱乐，消遣
duplicate [ˈdjuːplɪkət] *adj.* 复制的，副本的
maintenance [ˈmeɪntənəns] *n.* 维修
deposit [dɪˈpɒzɪt] *n.* 押金
key card [kiː kɑːd] 钥匙卡

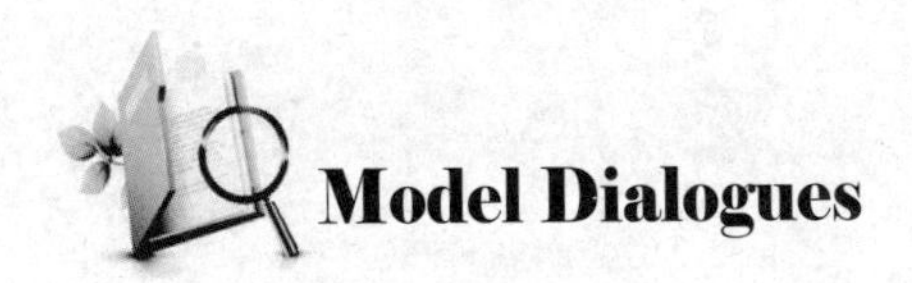

Model Dialogues

Dialogue 1

(Wang Qiang, a sales manager of Guangzhou Foreign Trade Import & Export Company, is checking in at the front desk of Hilton Hotel in New York.)

Receptionist: Good morning, sir. Can I help you?

Wang: Good morning. I have a reservation[1] for a single room here under the name Wang Qiang.

Receptionist: May I have your credit card and passport?

Wang: OK. Here you are.

Receptionist: Just a moment, sir. Yes, we do have a reservation for you, a single room for 5 nights from May 5 to May 10. Is it correct, Mr. Wang?

Wang: Yes, that's correct.

Receptionist: Would you please fill out this form while I prepare the key card[2] for you?

Wang: Sure. (After he has completed the form.) I think I've filled in everything correctly.

Receptionist: Thank you. Now everything's in order, Mr. Wang. Your room number is 1420. It is on the 14th floor. Here is your key card. Breakfast is from 7:00 to 10:00 a.m. and checkout is before 12:00 at noon.

Wang: Thank you very much.

Receptionist: And now if you are ready, Mr. Wang, I'll call the bellboy[3] to help you with your luggage.

Wang: Yes, I'm ready. Thank you.

Receptionist: I hope you'll enjoy your stay with us.

Wang: Thank you. I will.

Notes:

[1] reservation 也可以用 booking，是指预订。

[2] key card 是指（酒店）房卡。

[3] bellboy 也作 bellman，指旅店的行李员。

More to Learn for Dialogue 1

1. Arranging the room

(1) Can I take a double room with a front view/facing the sea?

(2) I'd like a quiet room away from the street if possible.

(3) Can you arrange a non-smoking room for me?

2. Hotel services

(1) — I wonder if it is possible for me to extend my stay at this hotel for two days.

— I'll take a look at the hotel's booking status.

(2) — Is there any place in the hotel where we can amuse ourselves?

— There is a recreation center on the ground floor.

(3) — I wonder if your hotel has the morning call service.

— When do you want me to wake you up, sir?

(4) If you need anything else, please call room service.

3. Make a complaint

(1) Can you change the room for me? It's too noisy.

(2) There seems to be something wrong with the toilet.

(3) The toilet isn't flushed. Oh, it's clogged.

(4) The water tap drips all night long.

(5) I've locked myself out of the room. May I borrow a duplicate key?

(6) I'm sorry. May I have a look at it?

(7) I'll send an electrician from the maintenance department.

Dialogue 2

(Wang Qiang, a sales manager of Shanghai Foreign Trade Import & Export Company, is checking out at the front desk of Hilton Hotel in New York.)

Receptionist: Good morning, sir. Can I help you?

Wang: I'd like to check out now.

Receptionist: Your key card, please?

Wang: Room 1420, please.

Receptionist: Yes, Mr. Wang. Have you used any hotel service?

Wang: No, I haven't used any service.

Receptionist: Fine. This is your bill, Mr. Wang. Five nights at 90 US dollars each which makes a total of 450 US dollars.

Wang: Can I pay by credit card?

Receptionist: Certainly. May I have your card, please?

Wang: Here you are.

Receptionist: Please sign your name here.

Wang: OK. Is it possible to store my luggage[1] here until I'm ready to leave this afternoon? I'd like to say good-bye to some of my friends.

Receptionist: Yes, we'll keep it for you. How many pieces of your luggage?

Wang: Just three. I'll be back by 3:00 p.m.

Receptionist: That's fine. Have a nice day.

Wang: Thank you. See you later.

Notes:

luggage 是集合名词，复数形式不能直接加 s，而是要在前面使用 pieces of 修饰。例如：How many pieces of your luggage?（您有几件行李？）

More to Learn for Dialogue 2

Check out

(1) I would like to check out. Tom Hiddleston in Room 1218.

(2) Sorry, I am not clear about this item. I didn't make any calls.

(3) Can I pay by credit card?

(4) Is there a fee for extending the checkout time?

(5) Here is my key card and the receipt for the key deposit.

(6) I need an invoice, please.

Practice

Practice One: Matching

Match the sentences in the left column with the correct responses in the right column. Each sentence has only one response.

A. Where can I have my laundry done?	1. There's a plastic bag in the bathroom. Just put your laundry in it. It will be picked up after I make the bed every morning.
B. Would you please tell me the daily service hours of the dining room?	2. I'm awfully sorry, sir. I do apologize, but we don't have any spare room today. Could you wait till tomorrow?

C. I feel rather cold when I sleep. Can you turn off the air-conditioner?	3. Yes, you may go to the lobby and buy it from the newspaper stand there. With the map, you can find your way around.
D. Let me help you with your luggage.	4. It's very kind of you to do so.
E. Can I get a tourist map in the hotel?	5. I'll tell you how to get there. This way, please.
F. Can you change the room for me? It's too noisy.	6. The air-conditioner is already off, madam.
G. Please show me where the lift is.	7. Certainly. From 7:00 a.m. to 10:00 p.m.
H. Is there any place in the hotel where we can amuse ourselves?	8. There is a recreation center on the ground floor.

A. ________ B. ________ C. ________ D. ________

E. ________ F. ________ G. ________ H. ________

Practice Two: Blank Filling

Fill in each blanks in English based on the Chinese meaning.

(1) ______________________________.
（请帮我把行李拿到房间。）

(2) We'll manage it, ______________________________.
（我们会尽力办到，但是今天我们没有空余房间。）

(3) I wonder if ______________________________.
（不知道你们酒店是否有叫早服务。）

(4) I'm glad that we'll be able to ______________________________.
（很高兴我们可以满足您延长住宿的要求。）

(5) I left my bag here, but I can't ______________________________.
（我把袋子放在您这里了，可我找不着取物牌。）

(6) Would you please tell me ______________________________?
（请告诉我餐厅每天的服务时间，好吗？）

Situational Practice: Creative Tasks

(1) The sales manager Zhang Tian is checking in at the front desk of Concorde Hotel in New York. The talk with the receptionist should include the following points:

- requirement about the room,
- confirmation of the date of check-out,
- morning call/dining time/hotel facilities/laundry service.

(2) The sales manager Zhang Tian is checking out at the front desk of Concorde Hotel in New York. The talk with the receptionist should include the following points:

- hotel services,
- pay in cash/by credit card,
- luggage room/touring/shuttle bus (taxi service).

(3) Suppose you are a guest in a hotel. Organize dialogues with your partner based on the following situations.

a. You forget to bring your key card.

b. You complain to the hotel manager about the problems in the room.

c. You broke a cup in the room accidentally.

Knowledge Zone

I. How to Book a Hotel Room

1. Determine your budget

Before looking for a hotel and making a reservation, you need to ensure the hotel could meet your budget and your needs. This will help you to narrow down your search and shorten the time you spend in booking a room.

2. Think about your required accommodations during your stay

Consider how big you would like the hotel room to be, including how many beds you require and how many bathrooms.

3. Identify your ideal location or area

Sometimes, location can trump budget or required accommodations, especially when you are looking for a location that is convenient. You may decide to stay in a location that is central or downtown, which will allow you to access different parts of the city easily. Or, you may decide to choose a more secluded location so you have some privacy and can drive or walk to and from the main areas of town.

4. Search for hotels online

The quickest way to look for hotels is online through a hotel search engine. These search engines will allow you to specify your planned days of travel, how many nights you require, your ideal location, and your required amenities, if any. You can also specify how much you are willing to spend on the hotel.

5. Compare hotels using discounted search tools

You can also use discounted search tools to compare several hotel options at the same time. All you need to do is to specify your travel dates and your price points. These online sites will then search multiple databases for you and present several hotel options that best match your needs and that are discounted or offer cheaper rates.

6. Call the hotel to get a better rate

Calling the hotel directly can land you a last minute booking or a better rate. You may also be able to get a better sense of the customer service offered at the hotel. Try to call in the late evening, as the morning and afternoon are often busy for the front desk.

II. How to Behave as a Hotel Guest

1. Check in (and out) on time.

Are you ahead of the check-in schedule and will arrive sooner than expected? Do you need more time to pack your bags and check out of your room? While some hotel establishments have not-so-strict guidelines regarding early check-in and late checkout, never assume that it is alright to do so. Talk to the concierge if you cannot check-in and out on time.

2. Be polite to the hotel staff.

In one interview with time, a hotel general manager has this to say about good-behaving hotel guests: "The nicer guests are, the more they get." It truly pays to be polite. You'll find yourself being served by staff who are happy to see you and happy to do things for you. A lot of times, they will go the extra mile for you. That's primarily because you are polite to them.

3. Try not to use anything you don't really need.

A lot of things are already factored into your hotel room price, but this does not give us the liberty to consume the whole housekeeping cart to ourselves. Keep your consumption in check.

Do you really need it or do you just like to open it? Do you really need that much or are you just overwhelmed by the lavish stocks?

4. Hang the towels if you use it again.

In your home, you don't usually use one towel for just a day, and get fresh ones the next day, right? The same goes in hotels. Hang towels if they are still clean and you intend to use them again. For soiled towels, pile them up on the floor and have them taken care of by housekeeping.

5. Do not take away so much food from the breakfast buffet.

A complimentary breakfast buffet during hotel stays is heavenly. As you fill your stomach with good things, you'll soon reach a wall and will decide you can't take in more food. This thought enters your mind: should I ask for a goodie bag and pocket some for later? A muffin for the road, a yogurt for your child… Whatever it is, the key is in asking. Politely talk to the manager or the server if you can have some (not many) to go. They are more likely to say yes, anyway!

6. Keep the noise to a minimum.

Imagine lounging in the hotel garden, enjoying the peace and quiet you so long desired — but then a group of fellow guests come crashing in, talking loudly about the party at the bar the night before. You would not want to be in that scenario for sure, so you yourself must keep the noise to a minimum while in public areas at the hotel. This applies inside your room, too. So much noise and mindless activity can wake up or irritate the adjacent rooms.

7. Respect hotel property.

Treat the hotel as your second home. Surely you wouldn't roam around your own property and just cause havoc, right? Have the same mindset towards the hotel's. The worst thing that can happen is the establishment suing you for misuse of property. The worse — being charged for the fixtures and other assets you mishandled. Respect it as you would do to the property of your own.

8. Keep an eye on your children.

As you show good manners to other guests, part of it is keeping an eye on your children if you are bringing them with you during your stay. They may run around, scream their hearts out or explore the premises unattended, and the majority of people do not take delight in these situations. Furthermore, keeping an eye on them can stop the potential destruction of hotel property from happening. It is, of course, for the safety of your children, too!

9. Give tips to the hotel staff.

Here is a shortlist of hotel personnel that you should definitely tip.

(1) Valet and Parking Attendant, as you leave and give your car under his or her care.

(2) Bellstaff, as you arrive and depart.

(3) Porter, every time you have luggage to be moved.

(4) Bartender, depending on the beverage tab.

(5) Waiters, upon bill out.

(6) Housekeeping, during every cleaning visit.

(7) Room Service.

(8) Concierge, upon check out.

Late Check-out at a Hotel

Unit 4
Visiting a Factory

Learning Objectives

- Make a factory tour.
- Make a showroom tour.
- Make an introduction of the factory.
- Ask for and give information about a factory/showroom/workshop/product.
- Master the basic expressions of visiting a factory.

Warm-up Activities

Task 1

◆ Brainstorming:

Look at the pictures below. Can you recognize these in a factory? Tell them in English.

Task 2

◆ Discussion:

If you are a buyer who is going to visit the seller's factory, what will you want to know during your visit?

Task 3

◆ Group Presentation:

If a foreign buyer is going to visit your factory, what preparations should be made before the buyer's visit? Think it over and present it to the class.

Vocabulary

exhibition [ˌeksɪ'bɪʃn] *n.* 展览会

showroom ['ʃəʊruːm] *n.* 样品间，商品陈列室

recruit [rɪ'kruːt]	v. 招聘
discipline ['dɪsəplɪn]	n. 纪律
injection machine [ɪn'dʒekʃ(ə)n mə'ʃiːn]	注塑机
assembly line [ə'semblɪ laɪn]	流水线，装配线

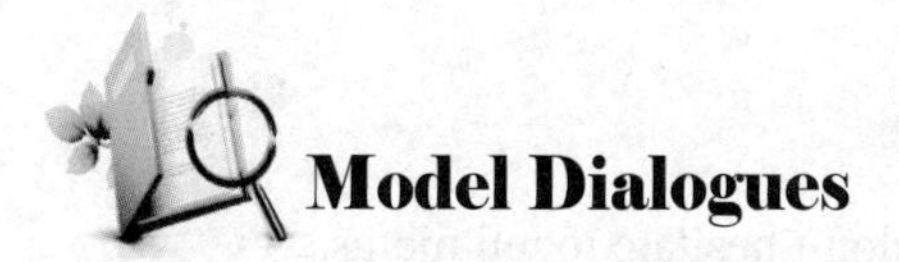

Model Dialogues

Dialogue 1

(Wang Qiang, a sales manager of Guangzhou Foreign Trade Import & Export Company, is meeting Mr. Smith, an Australian businessman at the gate of the factory.)

Wang: Good afternoon, Mr. Smith. Welcome to our lighthouse factory.

Smith: Good afternoon, Mr. Wang.

Wang: Mr. Smith, I think you've got my business card from the Canton Fair.

Smith: Yes, and this is my business card. I forgot to bring it last time.

Wang: Thanks.

(Mr. Wang's other colleagues also introduced themselves to Mr. Smith and exchanged the business cards.)

Wang: Mr. Smith, would you like to go through our schedule today?

Smith: Sure.

Wang: First of all, we're going to give you a brief introduction of our lighthouse factory in the meeting room. Then we'll move to the showroom to take a look at the product line[1]. Last but not least, we're going to take a factory tour[2]. Is it okay for you ?

Smith: Sounds great. I think after the factory tour, we need to go back to the meeting room to discuss some details of our cooperation.

Wang: Definitely.

Notes:

[1] product line 产品线

[2] take a factory tour 参观工厂

More to Learn for Dialogue 1

1. Before visiting a factory

(1) I've been looking forward to seeing your plant.

(2) I hope to learn a lot from this visit.

(3) You'll know our products better after this visit.

(4) If there is any place you'd like to stop by, please don't hesitate to tell me/us.

2. Introduction

(1) Would you mind meeting some of our colleagues?

(2) He was promoted to chief of the overseas sales department last year, so he is up to date with the European market.

(3) He's in the product development department. He knows more about this product than anyone else.

Dialogue 2

(Wang Qiang, a sales manager of Shanghai Foreign Trade Import & Export Company, is showing Mr. Smith around the factory.)

Wang: Let's go to the factory. This way, please.

Smith: There are six floors in this building. How many floors are used for production?

Wang: Floor Two to Floor Four are used for production. Floor Five is used for QA[1] tests.

Smith: What about Floor One and Floor Six?

Wang: Floor One is a warehouse for finished products[2]. The injection machines are also on this floor. All raw materials for production are kept on Floor Six.

Smith: Well, that's reasonable. How many workers are there in your factory?

Wang: It's around one hundred.

Smith: How many shifts[3] do they have per day?

Wang: Well, it depends. Sometimes two and sometimes three shifts per day.

Smith: What about the average delivery time of your products?

Wang: It's usually around 7 to 10 workdays for standard products. But for OEM[4] orders, we need around twenty workdays.

Smith: To be honest, your delivery time is a little bit long.

Wang: I agree with you. That's why we are updating our assembly lines recently to increase the output. I believe delivery time could be shortened in the near future.

Smith: Good to hear that. I think the design of some of your products are very suitable for our market. That's why I'm very interested in your company.

Wang: Thank you. Here we are at the assembly lines.

Smith: They look clean and tidy, and well-disciplined.

Notes:

[1] QA 的全称是 quality assurance 质量保证

[2] finished products 成品

[3] shifts 轮班制

[4] OEM 的全称是 original equipment manufacturer 原厂设备制造商，俗称代工，是指受托厂商按来样厂商的需求与授权，按照厂家特定的条件生产，所有的产品都完全依照来样厂商的设计制造加工。

More to Learn for Dialogue 2

1. Factory background

(1) — How big is the plant?

— It covers an area of one thousand and two hundred square meters.

(2) What's your annual capacity?

(3) We have five laboratories and a full-time staff of fifteen engineers.

(4) We're expanding our plant.

(5) There are 1,000 workers in the plant.

2. Touring a factory

— What's that building opposite us?

— That's the warehouse where the larger machine tools are stored.

3. Production

(1) In this plant, we produce about 15,000 units per month. We are running on three shifts.

(2) Is the production line fully automated?

(3) All products have to go through five checks in the whole process.

(4) This is the new conveyor belt we installed last year. We doubled our output in this department as a result.

4. Quality

(1) Quality assurance goes through all the processes from incoming raw materials to finished products.

(2) We will check each component before we install it.

(3) We're quite proud of our quality control procedure.

Practice

Practice One: Matching

Match the sentences in the left column with the correct responses in the right column. Each sentence has only one response.

A. How does your quality control system operate?	1. Very impressive, indeed, especially the speed of your NW Model.
B. Do you produce tools?	2. It's a pleasure to show our factory to our customers.
C. If I order a piece of X-ray apparatus today, how long will I have to wait for the delivery to Scotland?	3. This one seems a little small for me.
D. It was very kind of you to give me a tour of the place. It gave me a good idea of your product range.	4. I think you'd better speak to our factory manager, Mr. Smith. You'll meet him when we tour the factory.

E. That's the end of the tour. F. What's your overall impression? G. You'll have to wear this helmet for the tour. H. Could you give me some brochures on that machine? And the price if possible.	5. It is very informative. 6. All the products have to go through five checks in the whole manufacturing process. 7. Of course. Here is our catalogue and price list. 8. No, all the tools are purchased.

A. __________ B. __________ C. __________ D. __________

E. __________ F. __________ G. __________ H. __________

Practice Two: Blank Filling

Fill in each blank in English based on the Chinese meaning.

(1) We believe that ____.

（我们认为质量是一个企业的灵魂。）

(2) This is our ____________. Here is a full scale assembly of ____________ on display.

（这是我们的样品室。这里展出的都是我们的最新设计。）

(3) There has been ______________ for this kind of product.

（在我们的市场上这款产品有非常稳定的需求。）

(4) I think I've got ____.

（我想我对你们厂已有了一个大概的了解。）

(5) Do you have any difficulty in ____________________________________?

（在配合生产进度方面，你们有困难吗？）

(6) We've spent __________________________________, but it's better in the long run.

（我们在设备上已经投下巨额资金，但从长远看是有利的。）

Situational Practice: Creative Tasks

(1) Your company has specialized in electric appliances/textile/furniture for 10 years. A new client is going to visit your factory. You are required to receive the client at the gate of the factory.

Your talk should include the following points:

- small talk,
- introduction of yourself and your colleagues,
- a plan of the factory tour,
- factory background.

(2) During a/an electric appliances/textile/furniture factory tour, you give the client a detailed introduction to the factory. Your talk should include the following points:

- area of the plant,
- layout of the plant,
- shifts,
- product line,
- delivery time,
- quality control.

(3) Your client is very interested in how your products are so excellent in quality and how popular they are in the world market. Try to explain to him when visiting a factory.

Knowledge Zone

I. Key Benefits of Taking a Factory Tour

1. Relationships

Taking a factory tour is a wonderful way to build relationships with your suppliers and show them your seriousness about your project. Connecting personally and building great supplier relationships face to face can lead to better service, better pricing and better outcomes for your project.

2. Communication

Moving out from a purely transactional mindset and improving the way you connect and coordinate with your suppliers will lead to advantages in the speed and efficiencies of procuring products, reducing lead times（交货时间）and improving perfect orders.

3. Knowledge

Factory tours provide a powerful way to learn first hand how products are processed.

Talking face to face with the experts, seeing the materials and activities that go into the manufacturing process and witnessing the final quality checks can not only provide you intimate knowledge of that particular product, and the innovative manufacturing processes you witness may also inspire your thinking about your own working methods.

4. Assessment

Evaluating a supplier and the products they produce from a distance can be possible, but a factory tour will give you a clearer picture of the business.

You may already be familiar with the product range, but the benefit of a site visit to the factory enables you to see — from the inside — the way the business works, how they manage their processes, how the production runs, what their quality management looks like and how sustainable and responsible their manufacturing is.

5. Negotiation

Strong negotiation creates the difference between a successful budget project and a failed one. That could be better to negotiate with a potential supplier in person during a factory tour.

As Ed Brodow, negotiation expert, says "Negotiators are detectives." They ask the right questions and amass the right information to ensure they get the best deal. Knowing who you are dealing with and understanding their business personally will lead to smarter deals that benefit your project.

II. Midea factories join Global Lighthouse Network

Midea Group Co., Ltd. was honoured as a pioneer of Industry 4.0 technologies with two factories, Midea Hefei and Midea Jingzhou, included in the Global Lighthouse Network of the World Economic Forum (WEF), showing the Group's efforts in achieving both production efficiency and sustainability.

The Global Lighthouse Network is a community of production sites and value chains which are world leaders in the adoption and integration of the cutting-edge technologies of the Fourth Industrial Revolution (4IR). In total, Midea Group owns 4 WEF Lighthouse factories covering smart home appliances, which account for a relatively high proportion of the Group's revenue.

"Our factory used to produce high-end and middle-end products at the same time, and our production faced a very big challenge," commented Li Zhen, General Manager of Midea Jingzhou factory. "It was very inefficient in the traditional manufacturing way, and difficult to meet the needs of our consumers in time."

Through the implementation of the digital and intelligent transformation measures, Midea Jingzhou lighthouse factory adopted flexible automation.Technologies including the internet of things and artificial intelligence with more than 2,000 digital transformation initiatives have increased labor productivity by 52%, and reduced production lead time by 25%, the failure rate by 53%, and the utility consumption per unit by 20%.

Midea washing machine factory in Hefei has also witnessed a similar revolution. The number of product SKUs exceeds 1,100 and the annual production and sales volume of Midea Hefei is also at the forefront. "Digitalization has driven the transformation of our entire business process, model and increased efficiency," according to Zhang Zhimin, General Manager of the factory.

Targeting domestic high-end product segments and overseas market expansion, Midea Hefei Advanced 4IR Lighthouse factory widely deploys artificial intelligence and IoT (internet of things) technologies across end-to-end value chains to form a faster response and more efficient supply chain, resulting in lead time reduction by 56%, customer report defect rate reduction by 36%, and labor productivity improvement by 45%. Also, it helps to meet the goal of achieving carbon emissions peak in 2025 and net-zero in 2040.

"In the future, Midea Group will continue to increase investment in digitalization, IoT, global breakthroughs and technological leadership and invest in new cutting-edge technologies," said Simon Zhang, CIO of Midea Group.

As of January 2023, 132 Lighthouses have been identified from different industry sectors. China lives up to its moniker as the world's factory with 50 lighthouse factories, the most of any country.

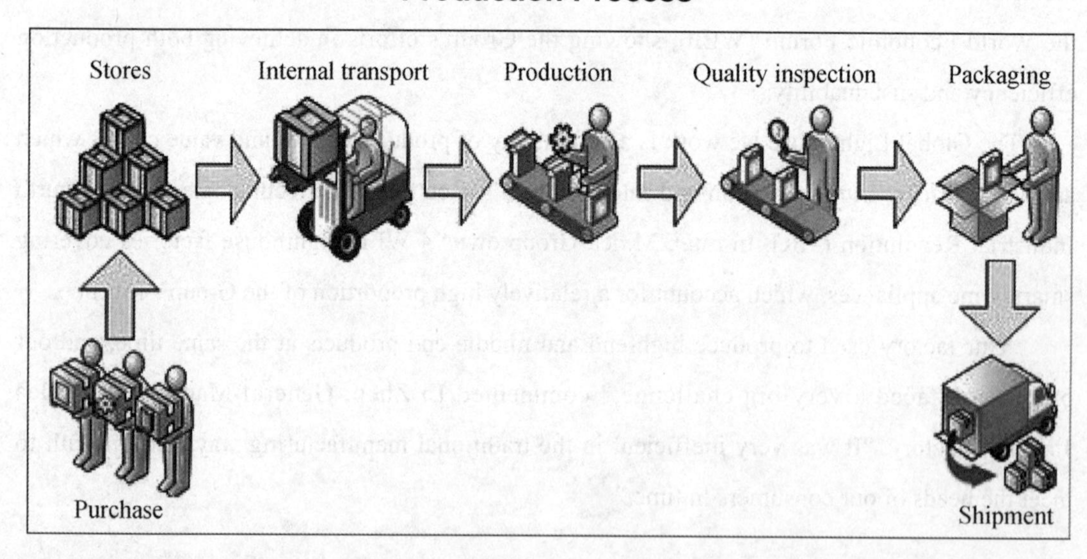

Unit 5
Introducing Products

Learning Objectives

- Welcome guests at the booth.
- Describe product specifications.
- Describe competitive advantages of products.
- Offer catalogues or brochures.
- Make use of some selling techniques.

Warm-up Activities

Task 1

◆ Brainstorming:

Look at the following pictures and express them in English.

Task 2

◆ Discussion:

If you are going to introduce a product to a potential customer, what aspects will you cover except for product design, technology, material and quality?

Task 3

◆ Group Presentation:

Choose a new product which you believe will sell well. Make a product introduction and present it to the class.

Vocabulary

customize ['kʌstəmaɪz] v. 订制，定做

waist [weɪst] n. 腰部

tutorial [tjuː'tɔːriəl] n. 教程

fabric ['fæbrɪk] n. 织物，布料

pattern ['pætn] n. 图案

renovate ['renəveɪt] v. 修复，翻新

exhibit [ɪg'zɪbɪt] n. 展览品

exhibition [ˌeksɪ'bɪʃn] v. & n. 展览

patent ['pætnt] v. 获得专利；n. 专利权，专利证书

circulation [ˌsɜːkjə'leɪʃn] n. 循环，流通

amplify ['æmplɪfaɪ] v. 扩大，增强

airflow ['eəfləʊ] n. 气流

decibel ['desɪbel] n. 分贝

execute ['eksɪkjuːt] v. 执行

represent [ˌreprɪ'zent] v. 代表

catalogue ['kætəlɒg] n.（产品）目录；v. 列入目录

electric fan [ɪ'lektrɪk fæn] 电风扇

ceiling fan ['siːlɪŋ fæn] 吊扇

floor-standing fan [flɔː(r) 'stændɪŋ fæn] 落地扇

bladeless fan [bleɪdlɪs fæn] 无叶风扇

trial sale period ['traɪəl seɪl 'pɪəriəd] 试销期

sample room ['sɑːmpl ruːm] 样品间

Model Dialogues

Dialogue 1

(Fang Qin, a salesperson of Qianjin Textile Manufacturing Company, is meeting a client named Ron Anderson at the booth.)

Fang: Good morning, sir. Welcome to our booth and this is my business card.[1]

Anderson: Thank you. Glad to meet you, Ms. Fang. This is mine.

Fang: What products are you interested in, Mr. Anderson?

Anderson: I'd like to see some silk scarves. I learned from some ads that your company manufactures and exports silk scarves to a wide range of countries.

Fang: You've come to the right booth.[2] China is the world's foremost silk producer. Our company has been a leading manufacturer and exporter of silk products for over 16 years. We specialize in silk scarves and enjoy great reputation in the international market.

Anderson: I am quite impressed by your exhibits here. They look classic and elegant.

Fang: Please take a look at this sample from our best selling line. It was a great success in the last exhibition in Guangzhou[3].

Anderson: Let me see. Oh, it feels soft and smooth, and the print pattern is unique. Is it made of 100% silk?

Fang: Quite right. 120 gsm[4] pure silk fabric. The shape and color can be customized upon requests[5]. Besides, the silk fabric provides health care to people's skin.

Anderson: Sounds great. Can it be worn around the waist?

Fang: Sure. It can be worn around the neck, the waist or a hat. It goes well with different outfits. Actually, each silk scarf is packed with a QR code card. If you scan the code, you will get a video tutorial demonstrating 15 ways to wear the scarf.

Anderson: That's wonderful. I'm really interested in placing an order under negotiation.

Fang: Great. We are looking forward to entering into business with you.

Notes:

[1] Welcome to our booth and this is my business card. 欢迎来到我们的展位，这是我的名片。递名片时宜微笑并双手递上，接过名片后应仔细阅读，可读出姓名、职位、所在公司等，也可以夸奖对方的公司、公司位置等。收下名片后最好放在名片夹里，切忌随意放置或在对方名片上涂写。

[2] You've come to the right booth. 你来对展位了。此处booth也可以使用stand表达相同意思。

[3] It was a great success in the last exhibition in Guangzhou. 它在上次的广州展览会上大受欢迎。此处 be a great success 可以理解为“大受欢迎”，还可以表达为 be very popular/be

met with great favor/be well received 等。

[4] gsm 此处读作 gram per square meter，译为克每平方米，gsm 是面料克重的一种表示方法，表示每平方米面料的重量。

[5] The shape and color can be customized upon requests. 形状及颜色能根据顾客需要进行订制。

More to Learn for Dialogue 1

1. Talking about product materials

(1) The product is made of 100% cashmere/silk.

(2) The new material is made from air, coal and water.

(3) Our line covers pure silk fabrics, synthetic and mixed fabrics.

(4) The yarn is carefully selected for quality and woven tightly in this fabric.

2. Talking about product competitive advantages

(1) We have improved our design to conform to the world market.

(2) Our products have gained a sound reputation for our fine craftsmanship.

(3) We offer a wide selection of colors and patterns.

(4) The pictures on the screen are clear, nice and steady. There would be no lines flashing on the screen.

Dialogue 2

(Liu Feng, a salesperson of Guangzhou Rainbow Fan Manufacturing Company, is introducing electric fans to his American customer, Mr. King.)

Liu: Excuse me, are you Mr. King from America?

King: Yes, I'm John King from New Jersey.

Liu: Welcome to our company, Mr. King. First, I would like to show you around our sample room[1]. This way, please.

King: Wow, the sample room is bright and spacious.

Liu: Yes, we renovate it and change the exhibits every two years to display the latest products. Here are some types of electric fans we have: the desk fans, ceiling fans and floor-standing fans.

King: Can you introduce this bladeless fan to me[2]?

Liu: Sure. The model number is EH505, one of our latest models. It is designed with patented air circulation technology[3] which amplifies the airflow in multiple directions. The bladeless design lowers the noise level to only 40~50 decibels. Besides, it is totally energy-saving, as it consumes only 50% energy compared to traditional fans.

King: Impressive. What about the quality[4]?

Liu: Absolutely reliable. Our company executes ISO 9000 in management and quality control of the products. This newly developed model has been strictly tested before we release it into the market. Here is the quality inspection certificate[5].

King: I'm still wondering if it can find a ready market in the US. You know, most consumers are doubtful about new products.

Liu: Well, our R&D team researched on customers preferences before we manufacture new products. We believe this bladeless fan represents the development trend for the next decade.

King: Can I have a catalogue and one price list? I need to study the products further.

Liu: Sure, here you are. Please feel free to contact me if you need any help.

King: Thank you so much! You've been most helpful[6].

Liu: You're welcome.

Notes:

[1] show sb around some place 带某人四处参观某地

[2] Can you introduce this bladeless fan to me? 能否为我介绍一下这款无叶风扇？

[3] patented air circulation technology 获专利的空气循环技术

[4] What about the quality? 质量怎么样？ What about 是用来征求对方意见的用语，可以用于询问信息、提出建议等。询问质量时也可以用 How is the quality?

[5] quality inspection certificate 质量检验证书

注意：电器类商品一般带有保修卡，保修卡一般用 warranty card 表达，在保修期内可以表达为 within warranty period 或者 under warranty。

例如：This electric fan is sold with a three-year warranty. 这台风扇的保修期是三年。

[6] You've been most helpful. 你帮了很大的忙。

More to Learn for Dialogue 2

1. Talking about product quality

(1) The quality is superior, yet the price is competitive.

(2) It is of prime/first class quality.

(3) You can rest assured that it is of fine quality.

2. Talking about product sales

(1) It sold remarkably fast during the domestic trial sale period.

(2) Digital cameras are enjoying fast sales these days.

(3) Our handbags find a ready market in your country.

(4) These products enjoy great popularity among young people.

(5) It has been the best-selling line of all time.

Practice

Practice One: Matching

Match the sentences in the left column with the correct responses in the right column. Each sentence has only one response.

A. Would you show me some electric fans?	1. Yes, I'd love to. I want to know more about its functions.
B. Can you make machines according to our special technical specifications?	2. Sure. Here you are.
C. How long is the warranty period?	3. No problem. We'll talk about the technical requirements before the negotiation.
D. You seem to be interested in our new Foot Massage Machine. Would you like to know more about it?	4. Yes, with pleasure. Which type do you prefer?
E. Have you looked into the sales?	5. That's a great idea. I'll take some home for our distributors.

F. Is the product reliable and durable?	6. Three years. If it's under warranty, you can enjoy free service.
G. May I have a price list with specifications?	7. Sure. We can guarantee that our product is of superior quality.
H. Let me get you a set of samples.	8. Yes. This product is gaining popularity in overseas market because of its fine quality.

A. __________ B. __________ C. __________ D. __________

E. __________ F. __________ G. __________ H. __________

Practice Two: Blank Filling

Fill in each blank in English based on the Chinese meaning.

(1) Our __________ products ____________________________________.

（我们的护肤产品在国内外都卖得很好。）

(2) I can __________ that ____________________________________.

（我可以向你保证，我们的产品是很有竞争力的。）

(3) The front-loading washing machines ____________________.

（滚筒式洗衣机有多种型号供您选择。）

(4) Compared with __________, our products ____________________.

（与同类型产品相比，我们的产品执行更严格的检测标准。）

(5) One of the merits of this machine is the ____________________.

（这种机器的优点之一是故障率低。）

(6) Our silk garments ____________________________________.

（我们的丝绸服装工艺精湛，设计新颖。）

Situational Practice: Creative Tasks

(1) Qian Feng, a sales representative, is meeting Mr. Cornell, a British business representative, to introduce silk dress/cotton shirt/nylon skirt. The introduction should include the following points:

• product materials,

• size and color,

• unique pattern.

(2) The sales manager Zhang Jin is making a product introduction to Mr. Wells, an Australian business representative, about a new model of floor-standing fan/rice cooker/microwave oven. The introduction should include the following points:

• product design/function,

• product quality,

• product sales.

(3) Suppose you are going to introduce a newly-launched TV set to your customer at the booth. Show the customer how the TV set works and briefly introduce its competitive advantages. Your aim is to impress the customer and push more sales. Create a dialogue and practice with your partner.

Knowledge Zone

I. Creating a Powerful Sales Presentation

A good sales presentation can influence customers to buy from you instead of your competitors. These 7 steps will help you create powerful presentations that impress customers and win the sales. The quality of your sales presentation will often determine whether a prospect buys from you or one of your competitors. However, experience has taught me that most presentations lack vigor and are seldom compelling enough to motivate the potential customer to make a buying decision.

Here are seven strategies that will help you create a presentation that will differentiate you from your competitors.

1. Make the presentation relevant to your prospect

One of the most common mistakes people make when introducing their product or service is to use a generic presentation. They say the same thing in every presentation and hope that something in their presentation will appeal to the prospective customer. I have been victim to this approach more times than I care to remember having been subjected to many “canned” PowerPoint presentations.

The presentation of your product or service must be adapted to each person; modify it to include specific points that are unique to that particular customer. If you use PowerPoint, place the company's logo on your slides and describe how the key slides relate to their situation. Show exactly how your product or service solves their specific needs. This means that it is critical to ask your prospect probing questions before you start talking about your company.

2. Create a connection between your product/service and the prospect

In a presentation to a potential client, I prepared a sample of the product they would eventually use in their program. After a preliminary discussion, I handed my prospect the item that his team would be using on a daily basis instead of telling him about the item I placed it in his hands. He could then see exactly what the finished product would look like and was able to examine it in detail. He was able to ask questions and see how his team would use it in their environment.

Also, remember to explain the benefits of your products, not the features. Tell your customer what they will get by using your product versus your competitors.

3. Get to the point

Today's business people are too busy to listen to a long-winded introduction. So it is essential to clarify your key points effectively and efficiently. I remember talking to a sales person who rambled at great length about his product. After viewing his product and learning how much it would cost I was prepared to move ahead with my purchase. Unfortunately, he continued talking and almost talked to himself out of the sale. Make sure you know the key points you want to introduce and practice verbalizing them before you meet your prospect.

4. Be animated

The majority of sales presentations I have heard have been boring and unimaginative. If you really want to stand out from the crowd, make your demonstration with enthusiasm and energy. Use your voice more effectively and vary your modulation. A common mistake occurred in people talking about their familiar products is to speak in a monotone. This causes other persons to quickly lose their interests in your presentation. I recommend using a voice recorder to tape your presentation. This will allow you to hear exactly what you sound like as you introduce your product. I must profess myself to be completely humiliated when I first used this tactic. As a professional speaker, I thought all my presentations were interesting and dynamic. I soon learned that my stand-up delivery skills were much better than my telephone presentation skills.

5. Use showmanship

In the book, *The Sales Advantage*, an example is given of how a vending sales person lays a heavy sheet of paper on the floor and asks his prospect, "If I could show you how that space could make you some money, would you be interested?" Consider the impact of this approach compared to the typical approach of saying something like, "We can help you make more money." What can you do to incorporate some form of showmanship into your presentation?

6. Use a physical demonstration

A friend of mine sells sales training and he often uses the whiteboard or flipchart in the prospect's boardroom during his presentation. Instead of telling his client what he will do, he stands up and delivers a short presentation. He writes down facts and figures, draws pictures, and records certain comments and statements from the discussion. This approach never fails to help his prospect make a decision.

7. Lastly, believe in your product/service

Without doubt, this is the most critical component of any presentation. When you discuss solutions, do you become more animated and energetic? Does your voice display excitement? Does your body language exhibit your enthusiasm? If not, you need to change your approach. After all, if you can't get excited about your products, how can you expect your customers to become motivated enough to buy your products?

II. "Made in China" Enters New Stage of "Intelligent Manufacturing"

As worldwide attention shifts to the 2022 FIFA World Cup in Qatar, the world's most famous enterprises have also entered a commercial race in which Chinese enterprises are one of the leading players.

According to Global Data, a Chinese data analysis and consultation company, Chinese enterprises have pumped around $1.4 billion into the Qatar tournament, making them its biggest sponsors.

In fact, "Made in China" is imprinted in more parts of the World Cup in Qatar. The Lusail Stadium, which is scheduled to host the final game, was designed and built by the China Railway International Group; the athletes' apartments are energy-efficient mobile houses built by a Chinese corporation in Guangdong province; the sewage treatment scheme was offered by a Chinese corporation in Shanghai; new energy buses introduced from a Chinese company in Henan province; the communication facilities at the stadiums and network equipment for the joint command and control center are all made in China; and 70 percent merchandise in surrounding areas of the race venues come from Yiwu in Zhejiang province. If the elements in the football field were contesting for a global manufacturing "World Cup", then "Made in China" would surely be a favorite to win the championship.

According to a recent World Economic Forum report, of the 11 global manufacturing "lighthouse factories" that represent the highest level of smart manufacturing and digitalization, five are from China. The first Chinese-made high-speed trains appeared on the Jakarta-Bandung high-speed railway line recently. A variety of heating items from China, such as cold-proof clothing, small appliances and electric blankets, are warmly welcomed in many overseas markets. Data from the China Association of Automobile Manufacturers show that in the first three quarters of this year, China's exports of new energy vehicles increased by more than 100 percent year-on-year. The technology of China's wind power equipment, Peta scale supercomputers and other products has risen to the forefront of the world.

With the accelerating integration of digital technology and manufacturing, Chinese industries will continue to climb up the high-end value chain, making "Made in China" enter a new stage of "intelligent manufacturing". Chinese manufacturing enterprises should strive to develop solid technical skills, increase added value, and attach importance to both local operation and the extension of the global coordination network, to expand the influence of "Made in China".

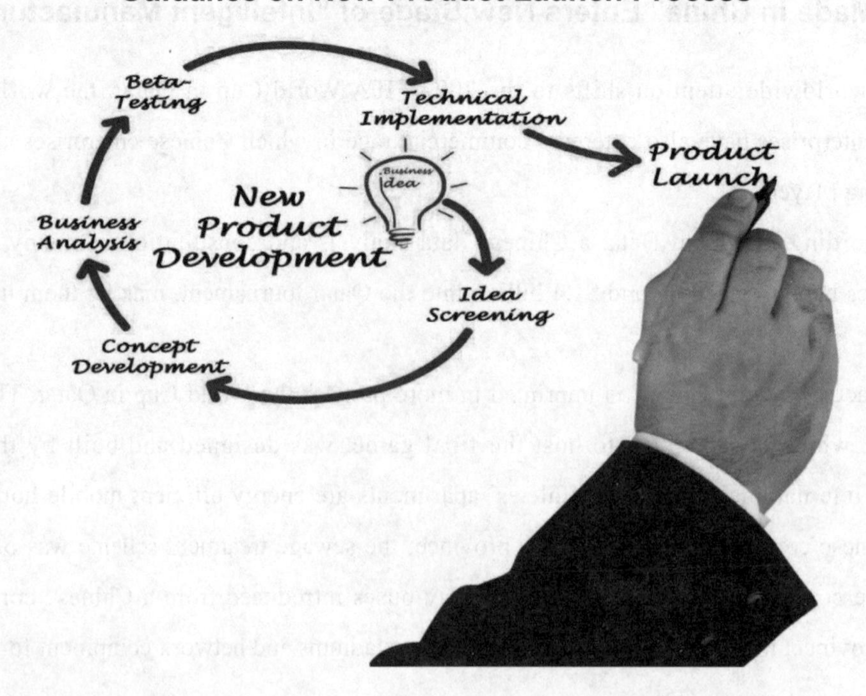

Unit 6
Price Negotiation

Learning Objectives

- Inquire about products.
- Quote different price terms.
- Adjust the price to conclude business.
- Practice key expressions in price negotiation.
- Master some negotiation skills.

Warm-up Activities

Task 1

◆ Brainstorming:

Product prices are affected by many different factors. Think of four factors affecting prices and share with the class.

Expressions of Price

英文术语	中文翻译	英文术语	中文翻译
actual price	实价	wholesale price	批发价
base price	底价	prevailing price	现价
cost price	成本价	price calculation	价格计算
gross price	毛价	price structure	价格构成
moderate price	合理的价格	price limit	价格限制
net price	净价	price regulation	价格调整

Task 2

◆ Discussion:

As a salesperson in foreign trade, what preparations will you make for a price negotiation with potential buyers?

Task 3

◆ Presentation:

Choose two negotiation strategies and think about how they can be applied in a price negotiation. Present the negotiation strategies with specific examples.

Vocabulary

user-friendly [ˌju:zə 'frendli]	*adj.* 用户界面友好的
energy-saving ['enədʒi 'seɪvɪŋ]	*adj.* 节省能源的
frankly ['fræŋkli]	*adv.* 诚实地
elsewhere [ˌels'weə(r)]	*adv.* 在别处
timely ['taɪmli]	*adj.* 及时的
after-sales service [ˌɑ:ftə ˌseɪlz 'sɜ:vɪs]	*n.* 售后服务
exceeding [ɪk'si:dɪŋ]	*adj.* 超过的
rock-bottom [ˌrɒk 'bɒtəm]	*adj.* 最低的
article ['ɑ:tɪkl]	*n.* 物品，物件
embroider [ɪm'brɔɪdə(r)]	*v.*（在织物上）绣花，刺绣
well-received [wel rɪ'si:vd]	*adj.* 受欢迎的
modest ['mɒdɪst]	*adj.* 些许的，不太大的，谦虚的
immediately [ɪ'mi:diətli]	*adv.* 立即，马上
approve [ə'pru:v]	*v.* 批准
range hood [reɪndʒ hʊd]	抽油烟机
counter offer ['kaʊntə(r) 'ɒfə(r)]	还盘
leading technology ['li:dɪŋ tek'nɒlədʒi]	领先技术
raw material [ˌrɔ: mə'tɪəriəl]	原材料
trial order ['traɪəl 'ɔ:də(r)]	试订单
repeated order [rɪ'pi:tɪd 'ɔ:də(r)]	复购订单
regular client ['regjələ(r) 'klaiənt]	常年客户
subject to [səb'dʒekt tu]	受……影响的
head office [ˌhed 'ɒfɪs]	总公司

Model Dialogues

Dialogue 1

(Ellen Huang, a salesperson of ATLAN Electrical Appliance Company, is having a

price negotiation with Joe Smith, a purchasing manager from ANC company in New York.)

Huang: Please take your seat, Mr. Smith. Would you like something to drink? Do you prefer tea or coffee?

Smith: Coffee, please. Thank you.

Huang: After attending our exhibition, could you tell me what kinds of products you are interested in?

Smith: Well, I've found the latest model of your range hoods standing out in the exhibition. And I want to set the ball rolling[1] by talking about its price.

Huang: Sure, let's get down to business.[2] The unit price of model EH-307 is USD 320, CIF New York.

Smith: I'm afraid your price is so high that we can hardly make a counteroffer.

Huang: Better quality usually means a higher price. Our latest model is designed with leading technology, which is user-friendly and energy-saving. If you buy our new product, you will get quality.[3]

Smith: Frankly speaking, if your prices were just slightly higher than other suppliers, there wouldn't be any problems. The truth is that your price is 20% higher than what we were quoted elsewhere.

Huang: The cost of labor and raw material has gone up since last year. The new metal we use has increased the cost by 30%. Also, you need to consider our timely delivery and superior after-sales service.

Smith: I think it's unwise for you to insist on your original price. To help us develop a new market for your products, I wish you could reduce the price to 280 dollars.

Huang: I'm afraid we can't. A reduction of 20 dollars is the best we can do for the orders exceeding 5,000 pieces. It's the rock-bottom price due to the superior product quality.

Smith: A reduction of 20 dollars sounds OK. Although it's still higher than our expectation, we accept your offer and place an order of 6,000 pieces.

Huang: You really drive a hard bargain[4], Mr. Smith. Let's call it a deal.[5]

Notes:

[1] set the ball rolling 开始（洽谈）

[2] Let's get down to business. 让我们开始谈正事吧。

[3] If you buy our new products, you will get quality. 一分钱，一分货。

[4] You really drive a hard bargain. 你真会讨价还价。

[5] Let's call it a deal. 我们就这么决定了。

More to Learn for Dialogue 1

1. Making inquiries/Asking about price

(1) What is the lowest price for it?

(2) Can you quote me the most favorable price?

(3) I'd like to have your quotation for this product.

(4) What is the unit price of this product?

2. Complaining about high price

(1) Your price is much too high/far too high/way too high.

(2) I'm afraid your price is on the high side.

(3) Your price appears to be higher than ever.

(4) The price of your products is rather unacceptable.

3. Requesting price cuts/discounts

(1) How much can you go down?

(2) I think this transaction would be more promising if you could make an appropriate reduction.

(3) Anything higher than this, we won't be able to sign the contract.

(4) Can you bring the price down a little?

(5) We wonder if you could give us a 15% discount.

Dialogue 2

(Liang Jin, a salesperson of Dannie Cloth Manufacturing Company, is meeting an American client named Ron Anderson at the booth. They are negotiating about discounts.)

Ron: Mr. Liang, can I have your offers for all the articles listed here?

Liang: Of course. Here is the price list. Is there anything more you want to know about these articles?

Ron: Yes, I'm quite interested in your embroidered tablecloth. We placed a trial order of 5,000 pieces last year, and it was a great success in our market.[1]

Liang: The unique design of this tablecloth has made it a well-received item. It sells well both at home and abroad.

Ron: But the price has gone up by 10% from the price list. As we placed a trial order last year, we would like to know what discount you'll offer for repeated orders[2].

Liang: Our usual practice is a 5% discount for regular clients, so it will be USD 190 per piece. And the final discount is subject to the quantity.[3] If you place a large order, say, 10,000 pieces or more, the discount will be 10%.

Ron: A 10% discount sounds modest. If you can grant a 20% discount, we'll place an order of 12,000 pieces immediately.

Liang: I'm sorry but we are unable to offer such a discount. The highest we can do is 15%, that is, USD 170 per piece.

Ron: Do you quote FOB or CIF?

Liang: All the prices are on FOB basis, so the price is USD 170 per piece FOB Shanghai.

Ron: I'm afraid it's still beyond our expectation. I need to consult the head office to see if they accept the price. By the way, how long do you usually keep your offer valid[4]?

Liang: The offer will be valid for four days.

Ron: OK. I'll get in touch with you in a day or two.

Liang: We are looking forward to your reply.

Ron: Thanks for your time, Mr. Liang.

Liang: You're welcome.

Notes:

[1] It was a great success in our market. 它在我们的市场大获成功（卖得很好）。

[2] We would like to know what discount you'll offer for repeated orders. 我们想知道你们对于复购订单能提供什么折扣。

[3] The final discount is subject to the quantity. 最终折扣取决于订购数量。

[4] How long do you usually keep your offer valid? 报价的有效期多长？

对于这个问题，可以使用 The offer will remain valid/effective/open for four days（报价有效期为四天）表示报价有效，还可以说The offer holds good until…，报价有效期直到……（接具体日期）。

More to Learn for Dialogue 2

1. Making Compromises & Waiting for Notice

(1) Let's meet each other halfway.

(2) In order to conclude the deal, we'll make some concessions.

(3) We'll take the initiative to bridge the gap.

(4) I can't give you an immediate answer. I will consult the general manager.

(5) I'm not in a position to approve such a big reduction.

(6) I have to contact my head office and let you know their decision in a day or two.

2. Rejecting Price Cut/Discounts

(1) Our quality is far beyond comparison.

(2) Let's consider the top quality/timely delivery/superior after-sales service.

(3) You are driving it too close to our cost of production.

(4) Compared with the prices of similar products on the international market, our price has always been on the low side.

(5) Our price is already narrowly calculated and it leaves us only a small profit margin.

(6) Given its superior quality and a strong market, it still compares favorably with those you can get from other suppliers.

Practice

Practice One: Matching

Match the sentences in the left column with the correct responds in the right column. Each sentence has only one response.

A. I'm thinking if it is possible for you to take the responsibility of delivery to my company.	1. Sorry, I can't give you an immediate answer to this matter. I will consult the general manager.
B. Can you accept an order of 500 pieces? It is not a big one.	2. 4% off the original price.
C. How about the price terms?	3. I'm sorry to say we can't close business at that price.
D. If you could go a little lower, we'll place the order right away.	4. Sure, we can arrange for the delivery to you.
E. How much can you go down?	5. Thank you. That's a deal.
F. I think that your price is much too high, compared with those of other suppliers.	6. We'll be happy to accept your orders, no matter how small.
G. Because of the hike in the cost of raw materials, we were forced to adjust our price accordingly.	7. FOB price, with the port of shipment in Ningbo.
H. In view of our long-term business relationship, we accept your bid.	8. It's true that our products do cost slightly more than the other makers, but it's due to our technological superiority.

A. ________ B. ________ C. ________ D. ________

E. ________ F. ________ G. ________ H. ________

Practice Two: Blank Filling

Fill in each blank in English based on the Chinese meaning.

(1) Since we signed the last contract, ________________________.

（自从我们签订了上笔合同以来，天然气价格上涨了 3%。）

(2) Because of __________, I wonder ________________________.

（由于要额外增加一些推销费用，你们能不能稍微降降价？）

(3) Normally, we don't ____.

（通常情况下，对于小额订货我们是不给折扣的。）

(4) I'm afraid that there is ____.

（我恐怕没有多大的降价空间。）

(5) Our prices are ______________________, and it is ____________________.

（我们的价格与世界行情是一致的，是可行的。）

(6) Do you mean ____?

（你是说平摊价格差距吗？）

Situational Practice: Creative Tasks

(1) The sales manager Wu Jie is meeting his Australian client Karen Brown in the booth of a trade fair. Wu Jie is trying to make a deal with Karen. In the conversation, they should:

- greet the client at the booth,
- briefly introduce the products,
- make inquiries and offers.

(2) Yang Feng, an export sales manager of King's Import and Export Co. Ltd, meets a client Mrs. Doris at the Canton Fair. Yang Feng is trying to persuade Mrs. Doris to place a trial order of mobile phones. In the conversation, they should:

- introduce the competitive advantages of the mobile phones,
- complain about high price and make counteroffers,
- have a hard bargain and place a trial order of 5,000 pieces.

(3) The customer thinks there should be a big discount for repeated orders. However, as a salesperson, you should give reasons and insist on a 10% discount. You should make good use of some negotiation strategies if necessary. The intended result is to make the customer order 5,000 pieces of your product.

Knowledge Zone

I. Common Negotiation Strategies

There are four common strategies that are used in various ways. Here are details.

1. Yielding

A yielding strategy is to not negotiate. A person who yields to accept the first offer or assumes the price is fixed.

A common reason a person yields is to avoid inner discomfort from thoughts of taking advantage of someone else or the fear of breaking social rules that say you must accept what others say as truth. Another reason is fear of some form of conflict or other unpleasantness.

People who use the yielding strategy typically assume other people are more important and powerful than them, and so abase themselves by giving in at the earliest opportunity. They put gaining the approval of others well above getting what they want from the situation.

2. Compromising

A compromising strategy seeks some fair balance where both parties appear to get an equitable deal. A typical tactic people use is to “split the difference”, which is not necessarily the best way when the other person is using tactics such as highballing or asking for all needs, wants and likes.

People who use compromising tend to see others as worthy and equal to them, and hence seek fair play. They realize that nobody can get everything they want and seek an equitable arrangement. As with yielders, they care about what others think about them but have higher self-esteem and see themselves as equal to others rather than inferior.

3. Competing

A classic and more aggressive approach is to treat the negotiation as a zero-sum game where their goal is to get as much as possible at whatever cost to the other party.

People who take this approach often assume they are superior or feel inferior but need to appear superior. They may well use any of the negotiation tactics, including the more deceptive ones, and consider this is not at all wrong (after all, it is a negotiation). They may well generally distrust others, seeing the world as a dog-eat-dog place where you deserve what you can get and also deserve to lose what you lose.

4. Problem-solving

The problem-solving approach is closer to Compromising than Competing in that it starts from a position of respect for the other party. A person using this approach does not see the other person as a competitor or threat, but rather as a person who has legitimate wants and needs, and that the goal of negotiation is less to make trades and more to work together on an equitable and reasonable solution.

In particular, a problem-solver will seek to understand the other person's situation, explain their own, and then creatively seek a solution where both can get what they need. They will listen more and discuss the situation longer before exploring options and finally proposing solutions.

The relationship is important for a problem-solver, mostly in that it helps trust and work together on a solution rather than it being important that the other person necessarily approves of the first person.

II. Etiquette in Business Negotiation One Must Have

Business negotiations can be a complex balancing act. Etiquette in business negotiation is not hard to earn. With practice and attention, you can attain etiquette in business negotiation skills. Do not want to be pressed so hard that you are reluctantly putting the business away, but you also do not want to be so soft that you lack confidence and patience. Here are some suggestions for achieving etiquette in business negotiation skills.

1. Be genuine and respectful

Have a respectful attitude toward business partners, regardless of whether you are capable of holding a contract. This is the No. 1 rule of etiquette. Even though you need to explain your position firmly to the discussion or to persuade others to support your goals, this is not the time to laugh, mock, complain, attack, or hand over.

When you discuss, you are not just selling a product, promoting an idea or marketing your services — you are selling yourself. You want potential partners to see you as a sincere, honest and likable person who is easily approachable and easy to work with.

Express your sincere gratitude, be humble and do not beg for financial resources. The goal is to prove that not only is your product valuable, but your skills, passions, and skills are well worth the investment.

2. Be patient and listen

Take the time to listen. You might think you're in the hot seat — especially if your boss says you're in line to do the negotiating work — but don't rush the process. If you do not take the time to listen to other points of view, goals, and objectives, you may make incorrect assumptions.

Ask questions, such as “Are you expecting to get out of this discussion?” or “How do you think our company can help you achieve your goals?”

Take the time to listen, even if it tests your patience. You will probably learn something important in the process that can help you finalize a win-win deal.

3. Stick to your bottom line

Always know your bottom line before entering into business discussions. Otherwise, if you have to finish a meeting to reconsider your options, you will waste time.

Before going into negotiations, be sure to determine your desired outcome and make a pact — with yourself and others, if applicable — not to stray from it. Setting a bottom line will enable you to know when to step back from negotiations and when to move forward.

4. Knows when to back down

When the discussion gets heated, be gentle and go back. Angry words and threats undermine the negotiation process and often force business associates to respond defensively. Business negotiation etiquette always trumps ugly deal-making.

Try to re-establish common ground, review similar goals, and avoid being competitive or controversial. The main purpose of business negotiations is to find solutions that satisfy both parties. Nobody wants to feel like he’s got the raw end of the contract.

Do not offer an ultimatum or try to get the other party in a corner. You have to come in as a professional. If you approach the discussion from every angle and do not see a solution, be prepared to raise your head and move on.

5. Monitor international business etiquette

Research cultural norms before engaging in international discussions. Most countries have specific guidelines that guide business negotiations, and you do not want to risk offending anyone. For example, rank is very important in negotiating with Chinese partners.

In China, delaying meetings is viewed as disgraceful and humiliating. When working with French business associates, stick to a rigid agenda but keep a welcoming tone. Be clear, concise, and well-prepared to earn respect.

Guidance on the Collective Bargaining Process

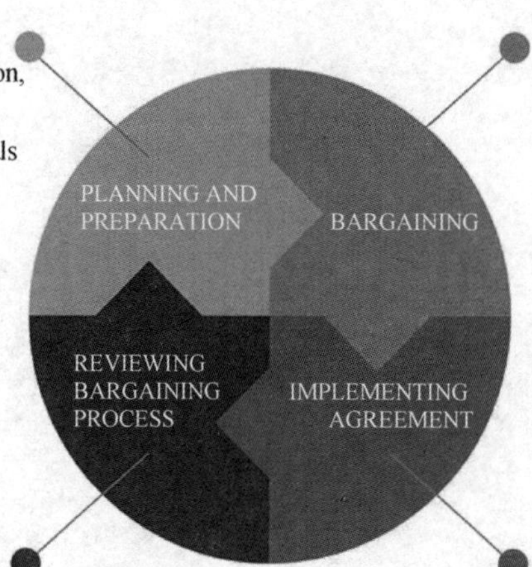

—Organizing bargaining committee

—Developing bargaining strategy

—Researching comparators, legislation, settlement patterns

—Developing a mandate and proposals

—Coordinating within the sector

—Establishing a bargaining agenda

—Negotiating

—Researching and preparing proposals

—Completing financial analysis of employer and union proposals

—Resolving roadblocks

—Concluding agreement

—Reviewing functioning of the team

—Analyzing barriers caused by relationship issues

—Reviewing adequacy of information

—Evaluating effectiveness of communication with stakeholders

—Drafting collective agreements

—Building a long-term relationship

—Identifying and addressing emerging issues

Unit 7
Terms of Payment

Learning Objectives

- Identify three major terms of payment.
- Tell the difference of frequently used terms of payment.
- Adopt suitable terms of payment in different situations.
- Learn the skills of persuading the other party.
- Master the basic expressions of terms of payment.

Warm-up Activities

Task 1

◆ Brainstorming:

What are the three major terms of payment in international trade?

Expressions of Terms of Payment

英文术语	中文翻译	英文术语	中文翻译
T/T	电汇	D/P after sight	远期付款交单
T/T in advance	预付货款	D/A	承兑交单
T/T on delivery	货到付款	Sight L/C	即期信用证
D/P at sight	即期付款交单	Time/Usance L/C	远期信用证

Task 2

◆ Discussion:

What are the main differences among the three major terms of payment? Discuss with your partners and make a list.

Task 3

◆ Group Presentation:

(1) What terms of payment will you recommend for new business partners? Why? Think it over and present it to the class.

(2) What terms of payment will you recommend for long-standing business partners? Why? Think it over and present it to the class.

Vocabulary

irrevocable [ɪ'revəkəbl]	*adj.* 不可撤销的
exception [ɪk'sepʃn]	*n.* 例外
consult [kən'sʌlt]	*v.* 咨询
guarantee [ˌgærən'ti:]	*v.* 保证
favorable ['feɪvərəbl]	*adj.* 有利的
inconvenience [ˌɪnkən'vi:niəns]	*n.* 不便，麻烦
monetary ['mʌnɪtri]	*adj.* 货币的；金融的
accommodate [ə'kɒmədeɪt]	*v.* 给……提供帮助
decline [dɪ'klaɪn]	*v.* （数量、价值、质量等的）下降
circumstance ['sɜ:kəmstəns]	*n.* 情况；环境
finalize ['faɪnəlaɪz]	*v.* 完成
concession [kən'seʃn]	*n.* 让步，妥协
facilitate [fə'sɪlɪteɪt]	*v.* 促进；帮助
tie up [taɪ ʌp]	套住，不能动用

Model Dialogues

Dialogue 1

(Wang Qiang, a sales manager of Guangzhou Foreign Trade Import & Export Company, is negotiating with Mr. Smith, an Australian businessman, about the terms of payment.)

Smith: Well, we've settled the issues of price, quality and quantity. Now what about the terms of payment?

Wang: We only accept payment by irrevocable L/C payable against shipping documents[1] when we deal with new clients.

Smith: I see. Could you make an exception and accept D/A or D/P[2]?

Wang: I'm afraid not. We insist on L/C.

Smith: To tell you the truth, L/C would increase the cost of our import. When I open an L/C with a bank, I have to pay a deposit. That'll tie up my money and increase my cost.

Wang: You can consult your bank and see if they can reduce the required deposit to the minimum[3].

Smith: There will still be bank charges in connection with the credit. It would help me greatly if you would accept D/A or D/P. You can draw on me just as if there were an L/C[4]. It makes no great difference to you, but it does to me.

Wang: Well, Mr. Smith, you must be aware that an irrevocable L/C gives the exporter the additional protection of the banker's guarantee. We always require L/C for our exports. When we import goods from our suppliers, it is our usual practice to pay by L/C.

Smith: Let's meet each other halfway[5]. What do you say if we pay 50% by L/C and the balance by D/P?

Wang: I'm very sorry, Mr. Smith, but I'm afraid I can't promise you even that. We insist on payment by L/C.

Notes:

[1] We only accept payment by irrevocable L/C payable against shipping documents. 我们只接受凭装运单据付款的、不可撤销的信用证。

[2] Could you make an exception and accept D/A or D/P? 你们能不能破例接受承兑交单或付款交单？

[3] You can consult your bank and see if they can reduce the required deposit to the minimum. 请你和开证行商量一下，看他们能否把押金减少到最低限度。

[4] You can draw on me just as if there were an L/C. 你就当作是信用证一样向我开汇票。

[5] Let's meet each other halfway. 我们都各让一步。

More to Learn for Dialogue 1

1. Ask about terms of payment

(1) — Could you tell me what terms of payment you usually accept?

— L/C at sight is normal for our exports to Europe.

(2) — Which term of payment shall we adopt this time?

— I suggest payment by documentary L/C for the present transaction.

(3) — Which method of payment do you prefer?

— We usually use L/C at sight.

2. Ask for alternatives

(1) — Is it possible to find alternative payment terms for this order?

— For a new client, we don't accept any other terms of payment except L/C.

(2) — Could you accept payment by D/P at 30 days after sight?

— All right. We will agree to change the term of payment from L/C at sight to D/P at 30 days after sight.

(3) — Do you accept a time L/C, say, 15 days after sight?

— We could consider your request.

3. Give reasons — buyer

(1) To open an L/C will add to the cost of our imports.

(2) When I open an L/C with a bank, I have to pay a deposit. That'll tie up our capital and weaken our cash flow.

(3) Our exchange quota is rather limited. We'd like to use D/A in this transaction.

(4) We have a cash flow problem this year, so I'd rather make the payment by D/P after sight.

4. Give reasons — seller

(1) L/C is the only term of payment we can accept when we deal with new clients. You know, safety is our first priority.

(2) As we all know, D/A might cause the sellers great trouble.

(3) Our company only allows us to receive payment by irrevocable L/C.

Dialogue 2

(Regarding the sample order, Mr. Carol, a British importer, tries to persuade Li Lei, a Chinese exporter, to adopt the payment by collection.)

Carol: Mr. Li, you see the world market has been rather dull recently due to the Covid-19 pandemic and we may easily get more favorable terms elsewhere, so we'd like to use D/A this time.

Li: I'm afraid we cannot accept D/A, as that can cause us a lot of inconvenience. As you know, the international monetary market is unstable. Therefore, we find it necessary to handle our business on L/C basis, at least for the time being.

Carol: But you know, opening an L/C is quite costly and will tie up the capital of our company. We do have a cash flow problem this year. What's more, I'm a long-standing customer and we have been cooperating well for years. I hope you can accommodate us in this instance.[1]

Li: But it is only under very special circumstances that we agree to other payment terms.

Carol: Ours is not a normal case, is it? It is under special circumstances and in the nature of sample order. It doesn't pay to adopt L/C for an order as small as ours[2]. The limited profit, if any, is not even enough to cover the additional expenses.

Li: Mmm… Well, in view of our long-term business relationship, we can exceptionally accept your payment by D/P at sight, though that's not our normal practice.

Carol: Thank you for your consideration. But it would help me a lot if D/P after sight is accepted, 30 days will be enough.

Li: I'm afraid no further concessions can be made. We make this concession just to facilitate your transaction this time[3].

Carol: All right. Let's call it a deal.

Notes:

[1] I hope you can accommodate us in this instance. 希望您能在此时多通融一下。

[2] It doesn't pay to adopt L/C for an order as small as ours. 这么小的订单无须用信用证支付。

[3] We make this concession just to facilitate your transaction this time. 就是为了促成您的生意我们才做出了这样的妥协。

More to Learn for Dialogue 2

Make a concession

(1) — How about meeting each other halfway, 50% by L/C and the balance by D/P?

— Well, I think we can make an exception for you this time. We will, as a special case, accept 50% by L/C and the balance by D/P.

or: — I'm afraid I can't. As I said, we require payment by L/C.

(2) We usually accept L/C. I've made an accommodation in accepting D/P, and I can't make any further concessions.

(3) In order to make a deal, we agree to D/P at sight. That is the best we can do.

Practice

Practice One: Matching

Match the sentences in the left column with the correct responses in the right column. Each sentence has only one response.

A. Do you accept D/A ?	1. Well, I trust you personally, but our company won't agree.
B. What are your terms of payment?	2. Well, if you send a technician to ensure proper operation and to offer after-sales service, we agree to make full payment by L/C at sight.
C. I'm a regular customer and we have been cooperating well for years, but you still have some doubts.	3. I'm sorry that can't be helped.
D. When shall we open an L/C?	4. No, I'm afraid not. As we all know, that can cause a lot of inconvenience to us.
E. How long should our L/C be valid?	5. We'd like you to pay us by confirmed and irrevocable L/C.
F. Payment by L/C is quite usual in international trade.	6. Thirty days before the month of shipment.
G. As an alternative, what do you say if we send a technician to ensure proper operation of the machine after arrival?	7. I know. L/C is all right, but could you consider 60 days' time draft?
H. The point is that opening an L/C does mean additional expenses.	8. The L/C should be valid for 15 days after the date of shipment.

A. ________ B. ________ C. ________ D. ________

E. ________ F. ________ G. ________ H. ________

Practice Two: Blank Filling

Fill in each blank in English based on the Chinese meaning.

(1) Payment by L/C ________ for us. This leaves us ________ at your terms of payment.

（信用证付款牵涉额外费用。按照你方付款条件，我们无利可图。）

(2) In order to make a deal, we can ________________, but that's not our usual practice.

（为了达成交易，我们就破例允许你们用即期付款交单的方式付款，但这并不是我们的习惯做法。）

(3) I hope you can ________________.

（希望您能在此时多通融一下。）

(4) In order to conclude the business, I hope ________________. What about ________________?

（为了做成这批生意，希望双方都各让步一半。百分之五十以信用证付款，百分之五十按付款交单怎么样？）

(5) Please indicate that the ________________.

（请注明信用证在我国可以议付。）

(6) Opening ________ and will ________ of our company.

（开具信用证的成本很高，并且会占用公司的资金。）

Situational Practice: Creative Tasks

(1) Mr. Richard, a Canadian buyer, is Mr. Wang's new client. They are negotiating about terms of payment (at least choose three terms to negotiate: T/T in advance, T/T on delivery, D/P at sight, D/P after sight, D/A, sight L/C, time L/C) for the transaction. The talk should include the following points:

- differences between the terms of payment,
- reasons for choosing the suggested terms of payment,

- (not) reach an agreement.

(2) Mr. Richard, an Indian buyer, is Mr. Wang's long-standing client. They are negotiating about terms of payment (at least choose three terms to negotiate: T/T in advance, T/T on delivery, D/P at sight, D/P after sight, D/A, sight L/C, time L/C) for the transaction. The talk should include the following points:

- differences between the terms of payment,
- reasons for choosing the suggested terms of payment,
- (not) reach an agreement.

(3) You are a sales manager of Guangzhou Foreign Trade Company. One of your company's regular customer introduces a client to you. In order to open up the client's market, what terms of payment can be adopted for the transaction? Make a dialogue with the new client.

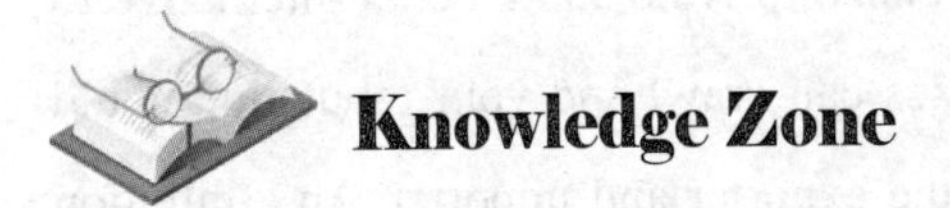

Knowledge Zone

I. Methods of Payment

To succeed in today's global marketplace and win sales against foreign competitors, exporters must offer their customers attractive sale terms supported by the appropriate payment methods. Because getting paid in full and on time is the ultimate goal for each exporter, an appropriate payment method must be chosen carefully to minimize the payment risk while also accommodating the needs of the buyer. There are five primary methods of payment for international transactions. During or before contract negotiations, you should consider which method in the figure is mutually desirable for you and your customer.

(1) International trade presents a spectrum of risk, which causes uncertainty over the timing of payments between the exporter (seller) and importer (foreign buyer).

(2) For exporters, any sale is a gift until payment is received.

(3) Therefore, exporters want to receive payment as soon as possible, preferably as soon as an order is placed or before the goods are sent to the importer.

(4) For importers, any payment is a donation until the goods are received.

(5) Therefore, importers want to receive the goods as soon as possible but to delay payment as long as possible, preferably until the goods are resold to generate enough income to pay the exporter.

II. What to do if your foreign buyer refuses to pay?

- Negotiate directly with the importer to come to an amicable solution.
- Reach out to the embassy/consulate or any other diplomatic presence of the importer's country in your country.
- Take the help of the concerned export promotion council in your country.
- Claim payment from the Export Credit Guarantee Corporation if you have an export credit insurance plan with it.
- Hire an international debt collection agency. Collection agencies work mostly through negotiation and rarely legal action, which means you have a chance of solving your payment problem without permanently ruining your relationship with the buyer.
- If all else fails, go in for arbitration, where a neutral third party resolves the dispute between you and your buyer. Arbitration is fast, cheap, private and a better alternative to legal action through the court system, where cases can crawl and your reputation could suffer. However, it requires the consent of both the exporter and importer. An arbitration clause can be included in your contract. Arbitration cases in international trade are handled by institutions such as the International Chamber of Commerce.

Payment Risk Diagram

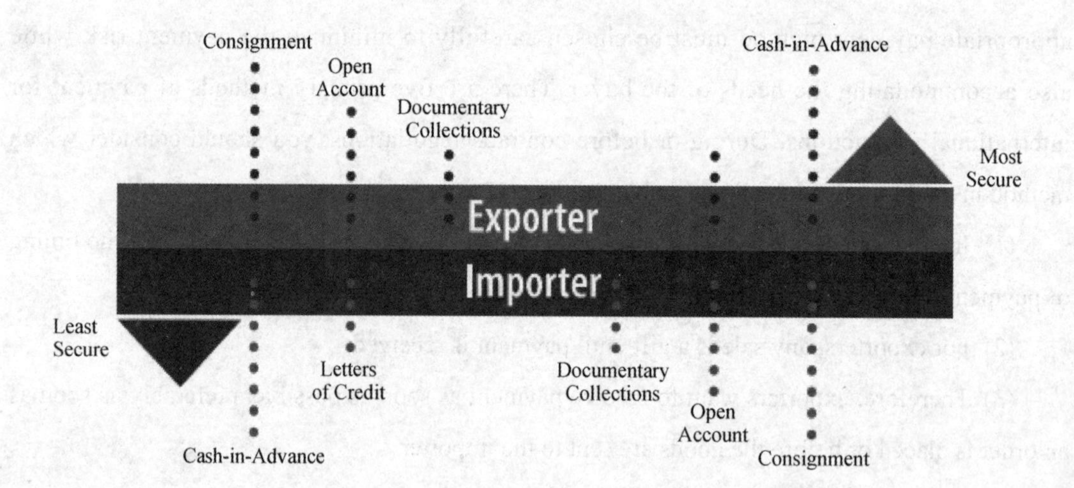

Unit 8
Shipping and Delivery

Learning Objectives

- Identify basic transport modes.
- Tell the differences of the frequently used transport modes.
- Advance shipping and delivery.
- Know how to make partial shipment and transshipment.
- Master the basic expressions of making a delivery.

Warm-up Activities

Task 1

◆ Brainstorming:

Look at the pictures below. What modes of transport are they? Tell them in English.

Task 2

◆ Discussion:

Which mode of transport is most widely used in international trade? Why? What are the disadvantages of this transport mode?

Task 3

◆ Group Presentation:

Which party, the buyer or the seller, do you think prefers timely delivery? Why? Think it over and present it to the class.

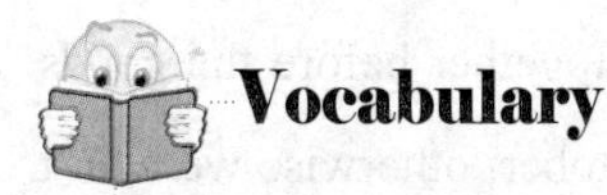

Vocabulary

settle ['setl]	v. 解决
commodity [kə'mɒdəti]	n. 商品
formality [fɔ:'mælɪti]	n. 正式手续
retailer ['ri:teɪlə(r)]	v. 零售商
commit [kə'mɪt]	v. 承诺，做出（错或非法的事情）
profitable ['prɒfɪtəbl]	adj. 有利可图的，有利润的
advance [əd'vɑ:ns]	v.（知识、技术等）发展，进步；n. 进步，进展
receipt [rɪ'si:t]	n. 收到
timely ['taɪmli]	adj. 及时的
backlog ['bæklɒg]	n. 没交付的订货，积压的工作
pilferage ['pɪlfərɪdʒ]	n. 偷窃
steamer ['sti:mə(r)]	n. 轮船，汽船
Madrid [mə'drid]	马德里（西班牙首都）

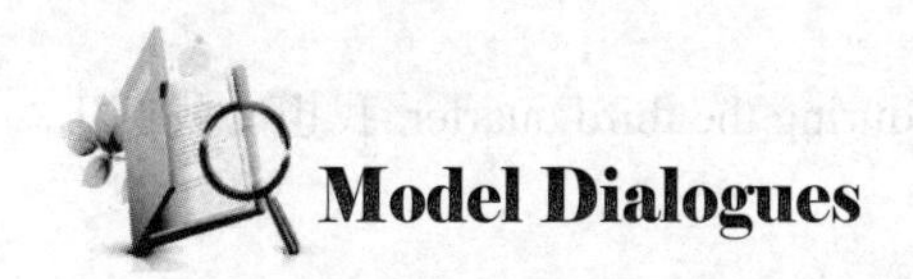

Model Dialogues

Dialogue 1

(Having settled all the terms of payment, now Mr. Johnson, an American importer, and Mr. Wang, a Chinese exporter, are talking over shipment.)

Johnson: Now we have settled the terms of payment. Is it possible to effect shipment[1] during September?

Wang: Sorry, I don't think we can.

Johnson: Then when can we expect shipment?

Wang: By the middle of October, I think.

Johnson: That's too late. You see, November is the season for this commodity in our market, and our customs formalities[2] are rather complicated.

Wang: I understand. I will see what I can do.

Johnson: Besides, after shipment it will be four to five weeks altogether before the goods can reach our retailers. The goods must therefore be shipped before October; otherwise we won't catch the selling season[3].

Wang: I'm afraid that our factories are fully committed during the third quarter.[4] In fact, many of our clients are placing orders for delivery in the fourth quarter.

Johnson: Mr. Wang, you certainly realize that the time of delivery is a matter of great importance to us. If we place our goods on the market at a time when all other importers have already sold their goods at profitable prices, we shall lose out.[5]

Wang: I see your point. The fact is that we have received more orders this year than any of the previous years. I am very sorry to say that we cannot advance the time of delivery.

Notes:

[1] effect shipment 装运，也可作 make shipment

[2] customs formalities 海关手续

[3] selling season 销售季节（不同的商品根据其特性销售季节不同，如空调的销售高峰是夏季。）

[4] I'm afraid that our factories are fully committed during the third quarter. 我担心我们工厂第三季度的生产任务已全部排满了。

[5] We shall lose out. 那我们就亏了。

More to Learn for Dialogue 1

1. Time of shipment

(1) — When can you ship the goods?

— As a rule, we'll deliver your goods within 15 days after receipt of your order.

(2) — How long does it usually take you to make a delivery?

— Generally speaking, we can make shipment in 30 days after your L/C reaches us.

(3) — When is the time limit for loading?

— The loading period is from July to August.

(4) Is it possible to effect shipment during April?

(5) — When can we expect shipment?

— By the middle of May, I think.

2. Negotiation on time — buyer

(1) It is too late for us to make shipment by the end of this month.

(2) October is the season for this commodity in our market.

(3) Our customs formalities are rather complicated. The goods must be shipped before October, otherwise we won't catch the selling season.

(4) A timely delivery means a lot to us.

(5) If we place our goods on the market after the selling season, we shall lose out.

3. Negotiation on time — seller

(1) Our manufacturers have a heavy backlog on their hands.

(2) Our manufacturers have a lot of orders to fill, so we cannot advance the time of delivery.

(3) We now have a rush of orders and we are working round the clock.

(4) Since you badly need a lot of goods, we need to book enough shipping space.

(5) I have to contact our producers to see if they can manage it.

Dialogue 2

(Mr. Johnson, an American importer, and Mr. Wang, a Chinese exporter, are trying hard to reach an agreement on means of transportation.)

Johnson: Mr. Wang, how about partial shipment? You can ship whatever you are ready in the early part of September.

Wang: Partial shipment? That is a good idea. But I have to contact my producers first.

Johnson: Can you call them now?

Wang: OK.

(After the call.)

Wang: Yes, we can ship the first half of your order in the early part of September.

Johnson: That's excellent. But I hope you won't make transshipment of our order, because transshipment adds expenses as well as risks of damage and pilferage [1].

Wang: That won't be the case. We can book the shipping space[2] on the direct steamer[3] to your port. There are 2 steamers from Shenzhen to Madrid.

Johnson: I won't worry about the first 50% of our order. Mr. Wang, how about the delivery of the balance[4]?

Wang: Well, we'll try our best to ship the rest by late september to enable you to catch the selling season.

Johnson: Thank you very much. I'd like to place further orders with you in future.

Notes:

[1] Because transshipment adds expense as well as risks of damage and pilferage. 因为转运增加了费用，也增加了损坏和偷窃的风险。

[2] book the shipping space 订舱

[3] direct steamer 直达船，也可以用 direct ship/vessel 表达。

[4] balance 余货

More to Learn for Dialogue 2

1. Negotiation on means of transport — buyer

(1) — How about partial shipment? You can ship whatever you prepare in the early part of October.

— That's a good idea. We can ship the first half of your order in the early part of October.

(2) I hope you won't make transshipment of our order because transshipment adds expenses as well as risks of damage and pilferage.

(3) In order to ensure the earlier shipment, we'd like to make this an exception and agree to transshipment.

(4) — If possible, partial shipment would be allowed. Because the selling season is coming soon, we have to catch the market. I really need your help, Mr. He.

— Considering the long-term business relationship between us, I must do my best to help you.

2. Negotiation on means of transport — seller

(1) We hope you agree to ship by installment.

(2) — There are not so many direct ships to your port. It's hard to book shipping space.

— It doesn't matter. We agree to transshipment.

(3) I'm afraid we can't ship the goods within this month due to the port congestion.

(4) Since there is no direct vessel, we have to arrange combined transportation by rail and sea.

Practice

Practice One: Matching

Match the sentences in the left column with the correct responses in the right column. Each sentence has only one response.

A. When can we expect shipment?	1. It is very considerate of you! Let's call it a deal!
B. I desire to know if it is possible to effect shipment during April.	2. By the middle of May, I think.
C. Can you find some way for an earlier delivery? It means a lot to us.	3. I'm sorry that's impossible. It would be very difficult for us to get the goods ready in such a short time.
D. We'll try our best. Anyway, we assure you that the shipment will be made not later than January.	4. I'm afraid we can't agree to that.
E. Please ship the goods in one lot in April.	5. We will make an effort to advance the shipment to early May.
F. Our people are most anxious about the shipment in October; so far they've heard nothing from you.	6. I am sorry we cannot effect shipment in April.
G. The goods have to be here in March, otherwise we'd be behind the season.	7. I understand. I'll try my best.
H. How about making Hong Kong the port of shipment instead of New York?	8. We're sorry for the delay. The trouble is that direct sailings to your port are very few.

A. ________ B. ________ C. ________ D. ________

E. ________ F. ________ G. ________ H. ________

Practice Two: Blank Filling

Fill in each blank in English based on the Chinese meaning.

(1) How long ________________?

（通常你方需要多长时间交货？）

(2) I hope that ________________ after you get our L/C.

（我希望你们能在收到我方信用证后马上装运。）

(3) Shipment should be made before October, ________________.

（十月底前必须交货，否则就赶不上销售季节了。）

(4) ________________ we can make is ________________.

（三月初是我们能够做到的最早交货日期。）

(5) We can deliver ________________.

（我们可以在八月份交一半货，其余的十月份交货。）

(6) We can ________________ to meet your requirement.

（我们可以交现货来满足你们的要求。）

Situational Practice: Creative Tasks

(1) Mr. Zhang, a sales manager of Toy Bears Import and Export Co. Ltd. in China, and his client Ms. Scarlett from Boston are negotiating about the time of delivery. The talk should include the following points:

- time of delivery,
- request for advancing the time of delivery,
- reasons for advancing the time of delivery,
- accepting/declining early delivery.

(2) Sam White, a foreign client, meets Ms. Liang, a Chinese seller, to negotiate partial shipment and transshipment. The talk should include the following points:

- reasons for partial shipment,
- arrange equal/unequal lots including time and quantity,

- reasons for transshipment or non-transshipment,
- intermediate port if transshipment is allowed.

(3) Your client placed an urgent order. Your factory has already operated around the clock, so both of you are negotiating about the time of shipment. Try to soothe your client and work out a better way to meet his needs.

Knowledge Zone

I. How Partial Shipment can Work in favor of Seller and Buyer?

Partial shipment is allowed under the UCP 600 article 31 unless specifically prohibited in the credit.

Partial shipment is commonly used when the buyer does not need the whole quantity at one shot, sometimes it is related to the financing situation of the buyer (no financing ability to pay for the whole batch of goods).

This type of shipment is used frequently when the buyer has the production plan in place that needs the goods to be delivered to him as per his manufacturing plan. The buyer may ask for partial shipment and can work under the same L/C, but this cannot mean that this is obligation.

If the buyer and the seller after negotiation decide to work with L/C, they must take into consideration the validity period of an L/C equals to the delivery period plus one month to avoid expiration.

So L/C should be valid for the entire period of goods offer and delivery. Goods payment for each shipment must be executed against document listed in the L/C one by one till the last delivery fixed in the agreement between the buyer and the seller. If an L/C expired for some reason and the delivery period was extended for some reason related to two partners (seller-buyer), next presentation and delivery would be considered invalid. But if the two parties still want to achieve the deal, the buyer can amend the L/C to extend the validity. All this depends on the relation formed between the seller and buyer. If they see that they can work together with no problem, they can extend any document and agreement as long as they wish.

II. Top Chinese Ports For Container Shipping

China manufactures or assembles countless goods for export across many industries. Not surprisingly, China is also the world's largest container market — and its ports play a crucial role in international trade operations.

With 150+ major ports and 1,800+ minor ports, China is a central point for the global supply chain network. Popular ports in China include Shanghai Port, Ningbo-Zhoushan Port, Shenzhen Port, Qingdao Port, Tianjin Port, Guangzhou Port, Yantian Port, Chiwan Port, and more.

1. Shanghai Port

The world's largest and busiest port, Shanghai Port manages more than 25% of global shipping.

With a deep sea port and river port, Shanghai Port oversees more than 2,000 vessels monthly. It offers integrated container services such as stevedoring, freight forwarding, storage and warehousing, distribution, port logistics, and cargo handling.

Shanghai Port is equipped to manage all kinds of domestic and international cargo, but its main imports and exports include coal, metal, steel, petroleum, and machinery parts.

2. Ningbo-Zhoushan Port

Ningbo-Zhoushan Port is the second busiest port in China and the third-largest port in the world. After the merger of Ningbo and Zhoushan Ports in 2006, the port is officially called Ningbo-Zhoushan Port.

Located in the Zhejiang province in Eastern China, Ningbo-Zhoushan Port is a deep-water port connecting 260 container routes and 600 ports. Due to its location in the middle of the Chinese coastline, Ningbo-Zhoushan Port is one of the most densely routed ports, especially for ocean containers transiting mainland China to and from the Pacific Ocean.

3. Shenzhen Port

Shenzhen Port connects South China to the rest of the country. It is the fourth-largest seaport in the world and the third-largest port in China.

The Kowloon peninsula divides Shenzhen port into two parts. The western port is a deep-water port connecting to inland waterways, while the eastern port is a natural harbor for larger container vessels. The port is also connected to Hong Kong–Shenzhen Western Corridor (SWC) for moving freight via road.

Handling 550+ vessels monthly, Shenzhen Port has 140 berths for managing container traffic. Top export items from Shenzhen include medical equipment, tableware, chemicals, machinery parts, and plastic molds.

Transshipment Concept

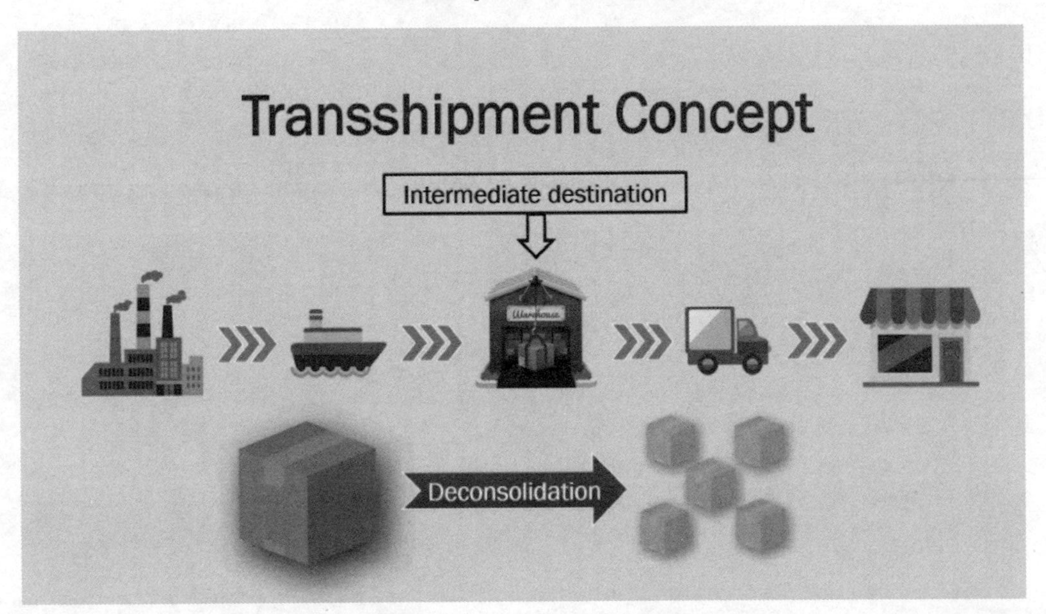

Unit 9

Packing and Marks

Learning Objectives

- Identify three types of packing.
- Tell the differences of three types of packing.
- Adopt different packing materials for different products.
- Know how to stencil shipping marks.
- Master the basic expressions of packing methods and materials.

Warm-up Activities

Task 1

◆ Brainstorming:

Look at the following pictures and express them in English.

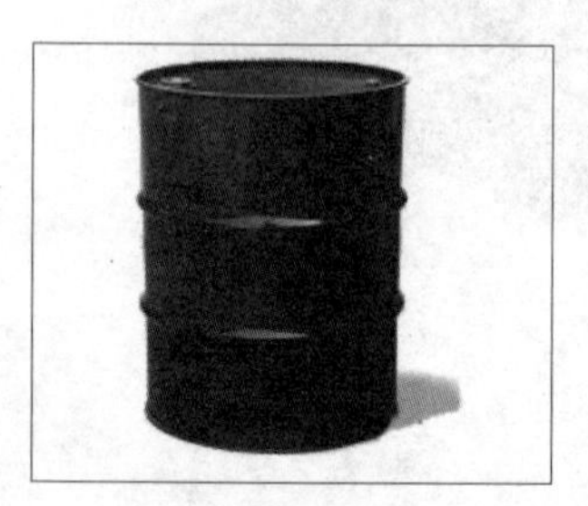
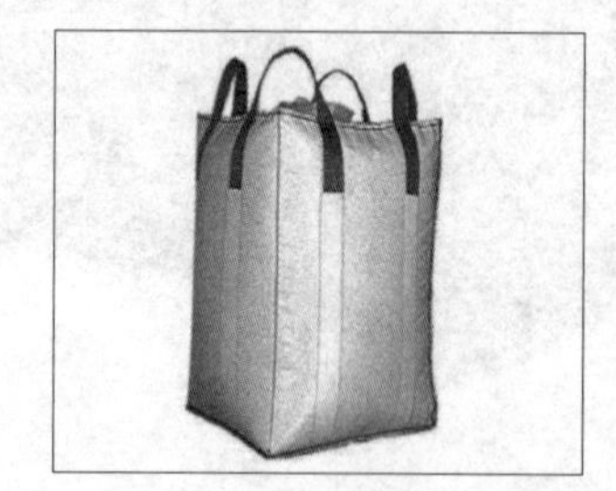

Task 2

◆ Discussion:

What are the advantages and disadvantages of the packing materials mentioned above? Make a list.

Task 3

◆ Presentation:

Identify the meanings of the following shipping marks. List the products and situations that are applicable, and then make a presentation to the class.

Vocabulary

packaging ['pækɪdʒɪŋ] *n.* 包装

merchandise ['mɜːtʃəndaɪs] *n.* 商品，货物

seaworthy ['siːwɜːði] *adj.* 适航的

voyage ['vɔɪɪdʒ] *v.* & *n.* 航行

nylon ['naɪlɒn] *n.* 尼龙

reinforcement [ˌriːɪn'fɔːsmənt] *n.* 加强

sculpture ['skʌlptʃə(r)] *n.* 雕塑品

jolting ['dʒəʊltɪŋ] *n.* 撞击

initial [ɪ'nɪʃəl] *n.* 首字母

stencil ['stensl] *v.* 用模板印制

be lined with [biː laɪnd wɪð] 衬有

polythene wrapper ['pɒlɪθiːn 'ræpə(r)] 聚乙烯包装

corrugated cardboard box ['kɒrəgeɪtɪd 'kʌbəd bɔks] 瓦楞纸箱

neutral packing ['njuːtrəl 'pækɪŋ] 中性包装

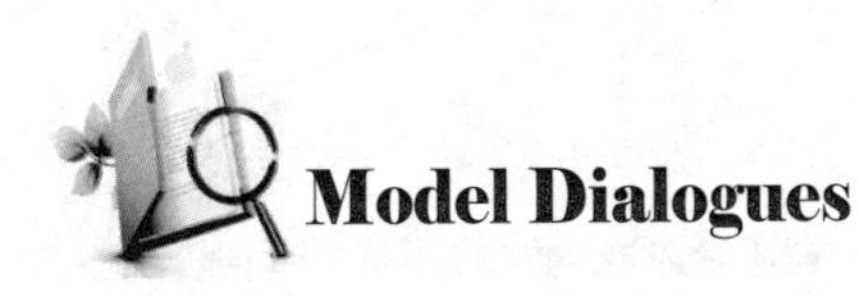

Model Dialogues

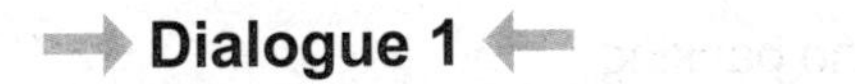

Dialogue 1

(Liu Mei, a sales manager of Guangzhou Foreign Trade Import & Export Company, is discussing the packing issue of shirts with Mr. John Brown, an importer.)

Brown: Mr. Liu, shall we now discuss the packaging[1]?

Liu: Very well. You know, we have definite ways of packaging. As to shirts, we use a recyclable polythene wrapper for each article, all ready for window display [2].

Brown: Good. Recyclable polythene wrappers are eco-friendly. Besides, A wrapping that catches the eye[3] will certainly help push the sales. With competition from similar producers, the merchandise must not only be of good value but also look attractive.

Liu: You are right. We'll make sure that the shirts appeal to the eyes.

Brown: What about the outer packing?

Liu: We'll pack them 10 dozens to one carton, gross weight around 25 kilos a carton.

Brown: Cartons?

Liu: Yes, corrugated cardboard boxes[4].

Brown: Are the cartons seaworthy? Can they stand long sea voyage?

Liu: You can rest assured of that. We'll reinforce the cartons with nylon straps.

Brown: That's good. By the way, do you accept neutral packing[5]?

Liu: Yes, we can pack the goods according to your instructions.

Brown: Great. OK, Mr. Liu, I'm now totally satisfied with your packing.

Notes:

[1] packaging 包装，尤指内包装

[2] As to shirts, we use a recyelable polythene wrapper for each article, all ready for window display. 至于衬衫，每件我们都用聚乙烯袋包装，这样可直接放在橱窗里陈列。

[3] catch the eye 吸引眼球

[4] neutral packing 指在商品的内外包装上未注明生产国别（如 Made in China）的包装。

More to Learn for Dialogue 1

1. Asking about the packing

(1) — We would like to know how you will pack the products.

— We'll pack the goods according to your instructions.

(2) I just want to know the details about the packing.

(3) Shall we now discuss the packaging?

(4) — Now the next thing I'd like to bring up for discussion is packing.

— OK. As this is the first time we have done business with you, we'd like to hear what you say concerning the matter of packing.

(5) I'd like to know the details about how you will pack the shirts.

2. Selling/inner packing

(1) The skin packing is the most advanced packing for this product in the world market. It catches the eye and can help push sales.

(2) As a rule, we use polythene wrapper for each article, all ready for the shelf selling/window display.

(3) I really hope that improving the package of the goods can further promote the sales of our products.

(4) In order to cater for the American consumers, we have asked the experts to design the inner wrapping.

(5) A packing that catches the eye will help us push the sales.

3. Transport/outer packing

(1) — What about the outer packing?

— We will use cardboard boxes with iron straps for reinforcement.

(2) I am afraid cartons are not strong enough for long-distance ocean transportation, since the goods are to be transshipped in Hong Kong.

(3) — We'd like you to pack the goods in wooden cases.

— As a matter of fact, you have to pay extra expense if you want to change into wooden cases.

(4) — How are you going to pack the goods?

— According to our standard practice, we normally pack them in cartons.

Dialogue 2

(Wei Qin, a sales manager of Shanghai Foreign Trade Import & Export Company, is discussing the packing issue of wooden sculptures with Mrs. Ellen, an importer.)

Ellen: Now let's move on to talk about packing. How would you pack the goods we ordered?

Wei: Each sculpture is packed in one carton lined with[1] plastic bubble wrap[2] to protect the goods from jolting.

Ellen: Do you think cartons are strong enough for a long voyage?

Wei: Don't worry. We strengthen cartons with metal straps outside.

Ellen: I don't think it's enough. The wooden sculptures may get damp during the long voyage. Could you use wooden cases lined with waterproof plastic sheets[3]?

Wei: We can use wooden cases lined with waterproof plastic sheets for packing if you insist. But this kind of packing costs more, and you have to pay for the additional packing. Besides, it will slow down delivery.

Ellen: But I don't want to take any risks. Besides, cartons are easy to cut open, which increases the risks of pilferage[4].

Wei: We could pack the goods in wooden cases lined with waterproof plastic sheets on the condition that you pay for 10% of the additional packing. And it will delay the delivery. You have to wait one more week.

Ellen: No problem. One more thing, could you mark our initials BTC on the outside of the cartons?

Wei: All right. We will stencil them on the outside of all the cartons. In addition, we will stencil on both sides of the cartons such words as "KEEP DRY, HANDLE WITH CARE".

Ellen: Also with the port of destination and our order number on it?

Wei: Of course. I can assure you that all the packing is made according to your instructions.

Notes:

[1] be lined with 衬有……

[2] plastic bubble wrap 塑料泡沫包装

[3] waterproof plastic sheets 防水塑料布

[4] Cartons are easy to cut open, which increases the risks of pilferage. 纸箱容易被割开，增加了被盗的风险。

More to Learn for Dialogue 2

1. Packing methods

(1) Ten bottles are put into a box and 100 boxes into a carton.

(2) They are packed in gunny bags of 60 kgs net each.

(3) We'll pack them six towels each with a different color in a box, ten boxes in a carton.

(4) Twenty of them make a carton, standard export carton.

2. Shipping marks

(1) On the outer packing, please mark the wording "Handle with Care".

(2) Each package should be marked with "Fragile".

(3) Can you put a country of origin mark on each carton?

(4) Please stencil our initials and order number on the outer packing.

(5) Can you mark them with wording like "HANDLE WITH CARE", "USE NO HOOKS" on each side?

Practice

Practice One: Matching

Match the sentences in the left column with the correct responses in the right column. Each sentence has only one response.

A. May I have a look at the packing samples?	1. Don't worry. The cartons will be well-padded and reinforced with double straps. They can stand a lot of jolting.
B. Could you stencil indicative marks like "Handle with Care" and "This Side Up" on the cartons?	2. Sure, we can mark the goods according to your requirements.
C. The goods will be packed in wooden cases. Do you have any other requirements?	3. No problem. Let's go to the sample room downstairs. This way, please.

D. I'm afraid cartons are not strong enough for long sea voyage. As you know, teapots are fragile goods.	4. Each carton will be lined with waterproof plastic sheets.
E. Dampness may get into cartons during long-distance shipping. How are you going to deal with it?	5. Yes, one more thing. The goods must be packed in strong wooden cases secured with iron hoops at both ends.
F. How are you going to pack those pliers?	6. They will be packed 20 pieces to a paper box, 40 boxes to a carton.
G. Are the cartons seaworthy? Can they stand long sea voyage?	7. Please go ahead and be more specific about that. I'm all ears.
H. The quality of your products is reliable, but your packaging needs some improvement.	8. You can rest assured of that. We'll reinforce the cartons with nylon straps.

A. ________ B. ________ C. ________ D. ________

E. ________ F. ________ G. ________ H. ________

Practice Two: Blank Filling

Fill in each blank in English based on the Chinese meaning.

(1) A: ______________________________?（箱子的尺寸是多少？）

B: Each carton is 30.5 cm high, 42.5 cm wide and 49 cm long.

(2) ______________________________, ten dozen to one carton.

（我们的衬衫通常每件单独装一个塑料袋，每十打装一个纸箱。）

(3) Packing must be seaworthy and ______________________________.

（包装必须适合海运，足够牢固，经得住“粗鲁”搬运。）

(4) ______________________________ and secured with metal straps.

（木箱子必须钉牢、加上压条并用金属条带加固。）

(5) As usual, ______________________________.

（跟往常一样，箱子要刷上一个菱形，里面写上我公司的首字母。）

(6) The design of the ______________________________.

（内包装的设计必须适用于橱窗展示。）

Situational Practice: Creative Tasks

(1) The sales manager Zhang Tian is negotiating with Mr. Mark, an Australian business representative, about the packing of tableware/rice cookers/toys. The negotiation should include the following points:

- inner packing,
- outer packing,
- neutral packing.

(2) Qian Li, a sales manager, is negotiating with Mr. Cornell, a British business representative, about the packing of bookcases/evening dress/pliers. The negotiation should include the following points:

- inner packing,
- outer packing,
- packing methods,
- changing outer packing,
- shipping marks.

(3) The customer thinks the cartons are not strong enough and intends to use wooden cases for outer packing. But in your opinion cartons are good enough for the lightweight articles and wooden cases would cost more. Try to persuade the customer not to change the outer packing.

Knowledge Zone

I. Main Difference between Packing and Packaging

Packing and Packaging are two activities that refer to the process of enclosing or protecting products for sale or transport. Many consider packing and packaging to be the same, but it is more accurate to consider these as two steps in the same process.

Packing includes preparing a product for transport and storage. Packaging includes preparing a product for storage, transport as well as sale. This means that packaging is also concerned with marketing and promotion, unlike packing.

This is the main difference between packing and packaging.

II. Two Key Advances in Green Packaging

Two of Huawei's latest packaging innovations have measurably cut CO_2 emissions and the wood used for transporting 5G MIMO products, helping to reduce the huge environmental cost packaging has on a global scale.

A green and sustainable approach to packaging is as important as protecting products in transit and smooth logistics. Huawei believes that the legacy problems limiting the widespread adoption of green packaging solutions can be solved by improved technology and processes.

Huawei's packaging teams use technology to reflect the company's long term commitment to simplicity, eco-friendliness, and recyclability when it comes to product design and packaging. Building on their progress in high-strength corrugated boxes, thin honeycomb paperboard, and other new materials, two of their latest innovations are multi-density cushioning technology using self-assembly expanded polypropylene (EPP) materials and lightweight plastic-steel pallets.

1. Multi-density Cushioning: Less Is More

Multi-density cushioning technology mixes raw materials of different densities into one mold. Starting in 2017, the packaging team in Huawei's MPE (Mechanical Power Environment) department began researching EPP materials that offer better cushioning performance but are recyclable.

The team mixed materials with two different densities in one mold to reinforce certain parts of the cushioning pad, identifying where the two materials should combine and how to control the composite interface using the mold. For testing, they ran different tolerances on a simulation model, including drop impact, vibrations from transportation, and stress limits. The resulting data contributed to the final design, which was then tested in a lab setting.

The technology is currently used for Huawei's wireless base station and server products. Providing the same protection as conventional single-density foam, multi-density cushioning reduces the packaging required by 38% for 5G MIMO products. In 2020, this technology reduced packaging weight by 1,362 tons — the equivalent of 2,165 tons in CO_2 emissions.

2. Lightweight Plastic-steel Pallets: Keeping the Wood for the Trees

Huawei's manufacturing department has a dedicated team for conserving resources in logistics. In 2019, they developed a new type of recyclable pallet for carrying products like wireless 5G base stations — the lightweight plastic-steel pallet. Traditional plywood pallets are disposable, easily breakable, and consume huge amounts of wood. The new lightweight plastic-steel pallets are not only more durable, they can also be recycled.

They're also up to 70% lighter. In 2020 alone, they reduced the total weight of Huawei's shipments by 4,739 tons, wood use by 39,500 m^3, and potential CO_2 emissions by 23,900 tons. Lighter pallets also lightened the loads being transported by truck, lowering gasoline consumption and carbon emissions.

In 2020, Huawei completed more than 300,000 shipments using these two green packaging technologies, saving more than 75,000 cubic meters of wood.

Huawei's packaging teams follow a "6R1D" green packaging strategy: Right, Reduce, Return, Reuse, Recycle, Recover, and Degradable. The strategy has helped Huawei build a green system that covers the entire lifecycle of its products, from materials selection, product design, packaging, and transportation to recycling and reuse.

Huawei's green packaging team believes that alongside its own efforts in developing biodegradable and recyclable packaging materials, more companies will follow suit and develop packaging techniques.

Guidance on Shipping Marks

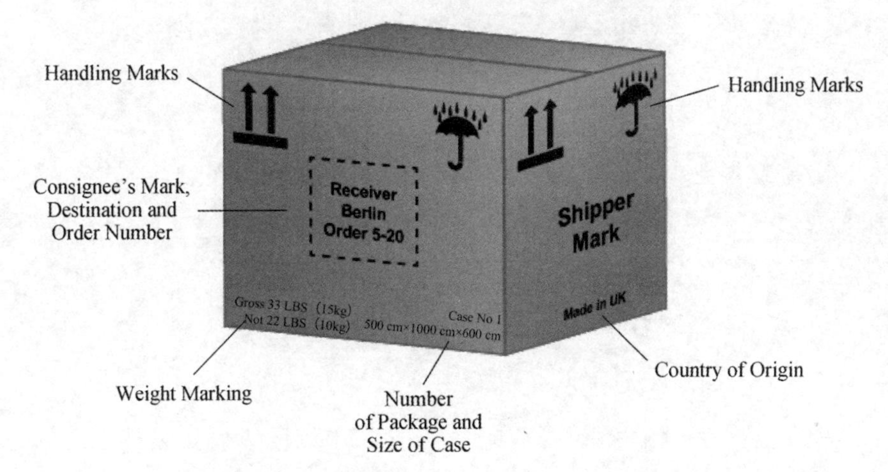

Unit 10 Insurance

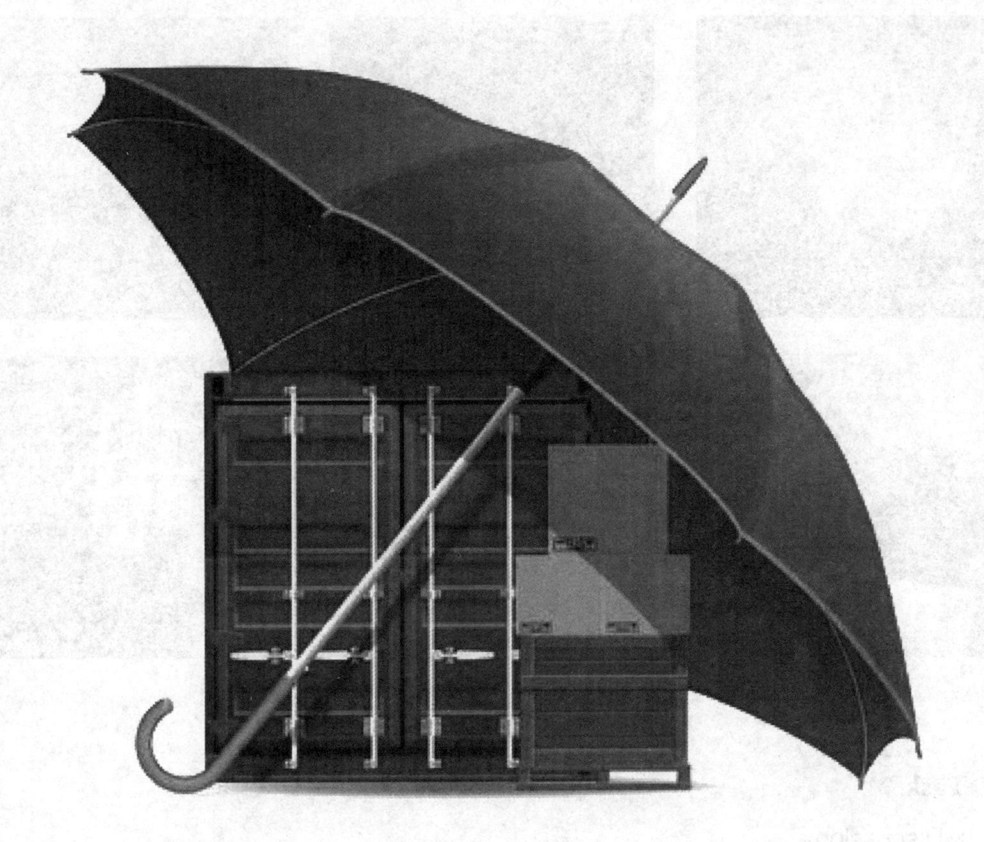

Learning Objectives

- Identify insurance coverage under CIC.
- Tell the differences between basic insurance coverages.
- Adopt suitable insurance coverages in different situations.
- Learn the knowledge about premium and insurance amount.
- Master the basic expressions of covering insurance.

Warm-up Activities

Task 1

◆ Brainstorming:

Look at the pictures below. What are these risks?

Task 2

◆ Discussion:

Among FOB, CFR and CIF, under which trade terms should the seller bear insurance costs? Under which trade terms should the buyer bear insurance costs? Why?

Task 3

◆ Group Presentation:

Which insurance coverage does the buyer prefer? Which insurance coverage does the seller prefer? Think it over and present it to the class.

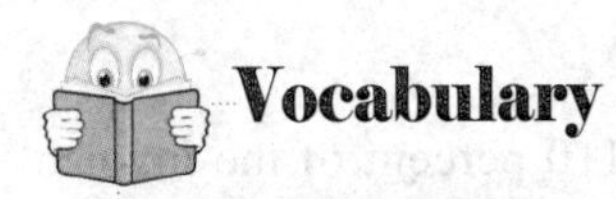

Vocabulary

cover ['kʌvə(r)] v. 覆盖；涵盖
coverage ['kʌvərɪdʒ] n. 险别（可数）；保险（不可数）
premium ['pri:miəm] n. 保险费
invoice ['ɪnvɔɪs] n. 发票
commencement [kə'mensmənt] n. 开始，毕业典礼
termination [ˌtɜ:mɪ'neɪʃn] n. 结束
excessive [ɪk'sesɪv] adj. 过多的，过分的

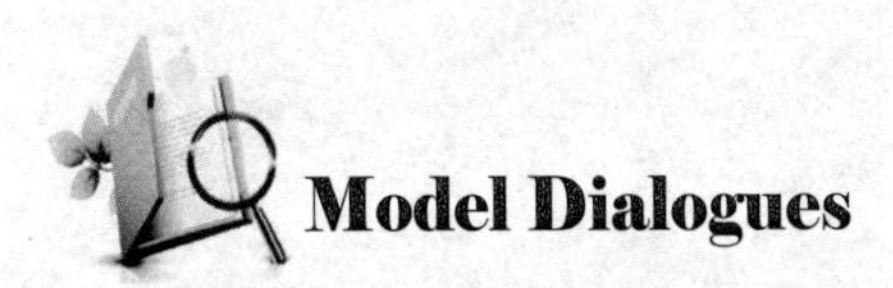

Model Dialogues

Dialogue 1

(Mr. Wang, an exporter of the Lucky Star Import and Export Company, is meeting his client Mr. Black, a manager from New York Sportswear Company, to negotiate about the insurance coverage.)

Black: What do your insurance clauses[1] cover ?

Wang: There are three basic coverages, namely, FPA, WPA and All Risks.

Black: If we conclude the business on CIF basis, what coverage will you take out for the goods?

Wang: Generally speaking, we only insure the goods against WPA.

Black: Do you cover risks other than WPA, for instance, TPND[2], Risk of Shortage and Fresh Water Damage?

Wang: Yes. If the buyers want to have the goods insured against these risks, we shall arrange for them.

Black: And it is the buyers who will pay for the extra premium, I think.

Wang: That's right. According to the international practice, we do not insure against such risks unless they are called for by the buyers.

Black: Another thing, we would like to have the goods insured for 130% of the invoice value[3]. Can that be done?

Wang: You know our usual practice is to insure the goods for 110 percent of the invoice value. If you insist on 130 percent of the invoice value, the premium for the difference between 110 percent and 130 percent of the invoice value should be put on your account[4].

Black: That's understood.

Notes:

[1] insurance clauses 保险条款

[2] TPND 全称是 Theft, Pilferage and Non-Delivery，意为偷窃、提货不着险。

[3] invoice value 发票价值

[4] put sth on your account 你方负担

More to Learn for Dialogue 1

Asking about insurance

(1) I'd like to get some information about insurance from you.

(2) Today I'd like to talk about the terms of insurance with you.

(3) —What risks do you usually cover?

—According to international practice, the seller just covers the lowest one, which is FPA.

(4) Do you cover risks other than WPA and War Risk?

(5) How long is the period from the commencement to termination of the insurance?

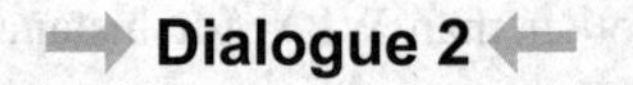

Dialogue 2

(Mr. Wang, an exporter of the Lucky Star Import and Export Company, and Mr. Black, a manager from New York Sportswear Company, are negotiating about the insurance amount.)

Wang: I am calling to discuss the level of insurance coverage[1] you've requested for your order.

Black: I believe that we have requested 25% above the invoice value.

Wang: Yes, that's right. We have no problem in complying with your request, but we think that the amount is a bit excessive.

Black: We've had many troubles in the past with damaged goods.

Wang: I can understand your concern. However, the normal coverage on goods of this kind is to insure them for the total invoice amount plus ten percent.

Black: We would feel more comfortable with the additional protection.

Wang: I see. If you want to increase the coverage, we will charge you extra premium.

Black: But the insurance was supposed to be included in the quotation.

Wang: Yes, but our quotation is for normal coverage at regular rates[2].

Black: I see.

Wang: We can arrange for the extra coverage, but I am afraid the additional premium is on your account.

Black: That's all right.

Notes:

[1] the level of insurance coverage 订单承保级别

[2] But our quotation is for normal coverage at regular rates. 但是我们的报价是常规税率下的正常险的报价。

More to Learn for Dialogue 2

Premium and amount

(1) — I want to know how much the premium is.

— It depends on the types of the risks.

(2) If you desire us to insure against a special risk, an extra premium will be charged.

(3) — What's the usual insurance amount?

— 110 percent of the invoice value.

(4) The extra premium for the difference between 110% and 120% of the invoice value will be on your account.

Practice

Practice One: Matching

Match the sentences in the left column with the correct responses in the right column. Each sentence has only one response.

A. I'd like to know what your insurance clauses cover?	1. Yes, we can. the Risk of Breakage is classified under extraneous risks.
B. How long is the period from the commencement to termination of the insurance?	2. All right.
C. Could you cover the Risk of Breakage for us?	3. 110% of the invoice value.
D. Who will pay the premium for the Risk of Breakage?	4. The coverage shall be limited to 60 days upon the discharge of the insured goods from the seagoing vessel at the final port of discharge.
E. What losses will be covered by All Risks?	5. It is 2% of the premium.
F. What is the usual insurance amount?	6. It includes FPA, WPA, and general additional risks, with special additional risks excluded.
G. We want to add the Risk of Breakage. What is the extra premium?	7. The additional premium should be put on the buyer's account.
H. Please cover the insurance for us.	8. We have three basic coverages, namely, FPA, WPA and All Risks.

A. ________ B. ________ C. ________ D. ________

E. ________ F. ________ G. ________ H. ________

Practice Two: Blank Filling

Fill in each blank in English based on the Chinese meaning.

(1) We have covered insurance on ________________ against All Risks.

（我们已将1000箱啤酒按发票金额的110%投保一切险。）

(2) If you desire us to insure against a special risk, ________________.

（如果您想投保特殊险别，我方将向您收取额外保险费。）

(3) ______________________________ suit your consignment.

（贵方货物适合于投保水渍险及破碎险。）

(4) According to __________, we do not __________ unless the buyers call for them.

（按照国际惯例，我们不投保这些险别，除非买方提出要求投保。）

(5) Which kind of insurance is ______________________________?

（哪种保险责任范围更广泛，平安险还是水渍险？）

(6) The insurance ______________________________.

（保险应该包含在报价里。）

Situational Practice: Creative Tasks

(1) A client named John Smith from Britain will discuss the terms of insurance with a sales manager from Buda Company in Guangzhou. The talk should include the following points:

- introduce FPA/WPA/AR,
- make a recommendation for insurance coverage,
- choose the right insurance coverage.

(2) Mr. Lin, a salesperson from Guangzhou, China, is going to discuss the terms of insurance against tea/cotton/garments with his client. The talk should include the following points:

- terms of insurance,
- choose the right insurance coverage: FPA/WPA/AR,
- negotiate about additional insurance amount/premium.

(3) Your Thai client is confused about three basic insurance coverages under PICC. The canned fish is exported to Bangkok where strikes break out from time to time. Recommend a reasonable insurance coverage to him.

Knowledge Zone

I. Negotiation Tips on Insurance

1. The more insurance coverage, the better

WPA coverage is too narrow for a shipment of this nature, please extend the coverage to include TPND.

2. Don't overpay insurance premium

As our usual practice, insurance covers general risks only at 110 percent of the invoice value. If coverage against other risks is required, such as breakage, leakage, TPND, hook and contamination damages, the extra premium involved would be put on the buyer's account.

3. Insurance clauses should be worked out step by step

You should study not only the benefits but also the terms and limitations of an insurance agreement that appears best suited to your needs.

4. Be careful to calculate insurance amount

10% above the invoice value is the usual practice in international trade.

5. Keep in mind the exclusions from insurance liability

Understand that the loss is caused by inherent vice or nature of the subject matter insured, which is outside the scope of the coverage.

II. InsurTech in China

Over the past decade, the digital economy in China has become a powerful growth engine for the country's economy as a whole. For the insurance industry, digital transformation — the integration of technologies throughout the value chain — has been a game changer. From organizational structures to business strategies, operations processes, product design and beyond, InsurTech has redefined how insurers do business, and will play an increasingly important role in promoting sustainable sector growth in the future.

To date, InsurTech is mainly used to boost sales of insurance policies and automate underwriting claims. Big Data and artificial intelligence (AI) are also being widely applied. Big Data in particular will play a key role in product innovation and risk pricing.

The InsurTech ecosystem in China consists of traditional and online insurers, internet and tech companies, and start-ups. All have different business strategies, and also have fundamentally different strengths and comparative advantages. This presents many growth opportunities. For example, tapping the digital capabilities and extensive user base of large internet companies can deliver exponential growth for insurers intent on designing innovative risk protection solutions tailored to specific consumer needs.

In the coming years, insurtech will further progress the transformation of China's insurance industry, by:

- enhancing product design through more flexible, diverse and customized features, which will accelerate upgrades and innovation cycles across the industry,
- enabling the cross-industry insurance ecosystem to customize insurance products to meet specific customer needs, and
- deepening the integration of technologies across the insurance value chain, which will make business operations more efficient and lower the costs of providing insurance, while also improving the claims experience and reducing the risk of adverse selection. Technologies will also extend the boundaries of insurability boundary. The benefit can pass on to consumers in the form of lower premiums which, with enhanced underwriting capabilities, will increase insurance penetration and help narrow protection gaps in the long run.

Trade Credit Insurance

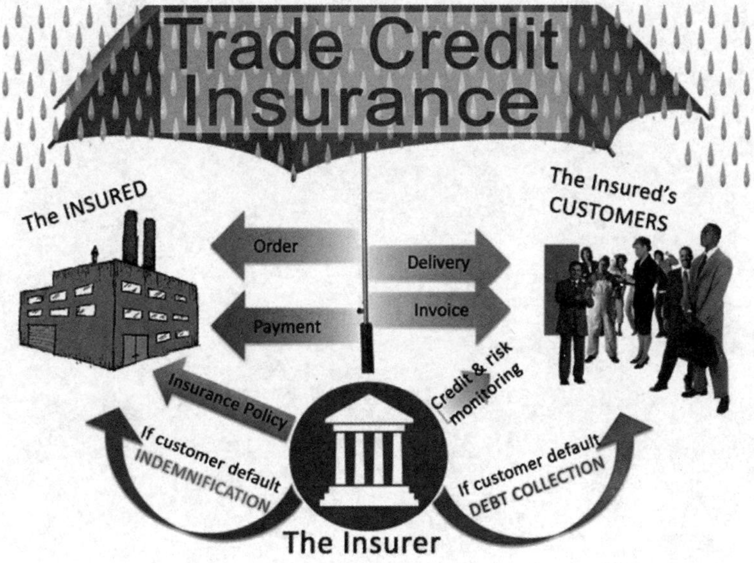

Unit 11
Signing a Contract

Learning Objectives

- Know the procedures before signing a contract.
- Identify important items in a contract.
- Discuss and amend a contract.
- Master the expressions of signing a contract.
- Learn the etiquette of signing a contract.

Warm-up Activities

Task 1

◆ Brainstorming:

What are the main categories of clauses in a foreign trade sales contract? (quality, quantity, packing, etc.)

Expressions of Contracts

英文术语	中文翻译	英文术语	中文翻译
make a contract	签订合同	Sales Contract, S/C	销售合同
draft a contract	起草合同	stipulations of a contract	合同规定
check the contract	检查合同	expiration of a contract	合同期满
amend the contract	修改合同	duration of a contract	合同有效期
in duplicate	一式两份	renew the contract	续订合同
in triplicate	一式三份	terminate the contract	终止合同
in quadruplicate	一式四份	cancel the contract	取消合同

Task 2

◆ Discussion:

Why is it important to examine a contract? Discuss with a partner.

Task 3

◆ Group Presentation:

If you are going to sign a contract with your business partner in your own company, what should you prepare and take into consideration? Think it over and present it to the class.

Vocabulary

tough [tʌf]	*adj.* 艰难的
draft [drɑːft]	*n.* 草稿
proceed [prə'siːd]	*v.* 进行，继续下去
valid ['vælɪd]	*adj.* 有效的
expire [ɪk'spaɪə(r)]	*v.* 期满，（期限）终止
clarification [ˌklærəfɪ'keɪʃn]	*n.*（意义等的）澄清，说明
inspection [ɪn'spekʃn]	*n.* 检查，视察
specify ['spesɪfaɪ]	*v.* 明确说明
schedule ['ʃedjuːl]	*n.* 时间表，日程安排
provision [prə'vɪʒn]	*n.* 规定，条款
duly ['djuːli]	*adv.* 充分地，适当地
review [rɪ'vjuː]	*v.* 检查，回顾
confusion [kən'fjuːʒn]	*n.* 不确定
upfront [ˌʌp'frʌnt]	*adj.* 坦率的，预付的
major ['meɪdʒə(r)]	*adj.* 主要的，重要的
observe [əb'zɜːv]	*v.* 遵守
loss [lɒs]	*n.* 损失
borne [bɔːn]	（bear 的过去分词）*v.* 承担
breach [briːtʃ]	*n.* & *v.* 违反
go over [ɡəʊ 'əʊvə(r)]	检查
be entitled to [biː ɪn'taɪtld tu]	拥有……的权利
initial order [ɪ'nɪʃl 'ɔːdə(r)]	首批订货

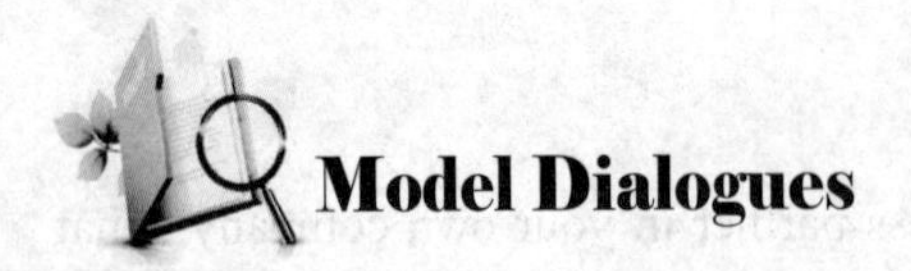

Model Dialogues

Dialogue 1

Reviewing the Contract

(Mr. Gao and Ms. An, the sales representatives of Guangzhou Eastern Star Company, are reviewing some important details of a contract with Frank and Muriel, the delegates from Fusions Company in Los Angeles.)

Gao: We've had some tough negotiations, but I think we finally reach an agreement. Here is the draft of our contract.

Muriel: Yes. If you don't mind, we'd like to go over the contract details one more time before we proceed.

An: Of course! Should we start at the top?

Muriel: OK, let's review. How long will this agreement be valid[1]?

An: As you can see here, the contract states that this agreement is valid for one year.

Frank: So when the contract expires in one year, will it be possible to be renewed?

Gao: Yes, if both parties agree to do so.

Frank: Now we would like to make some clarifications on the inspection of the goods.

Gao: As you specify, you will be able to inspect all items before you accept delivery. That has been included in the contract, too.

Muriel: And that's for all shipments, correct?

An: Correct. As for the shipping schedule, we've set up monthly shipment at the end of each month for the one year period of the contract.

Frank: If this schedule ever changes, we will need a notice at least two months in advance[2].

Gao: Certainly. This provision has been duly noted in the contract[3]. Is there anything else we should go over?

Muriel: Let's review the terms of payment one more time, just to avoid any possible confusions in the future.

An: Good idea! I stated in the contract a payment of USD 10,000 will be made in advance on initial order.

Frank: We understand that. But could you walk us through the fine print[4]?

An: Sure. Once this payment has been received, the order will be shipped. The rest of the payment must then be made when you receive and accept the shipment.

Frank: That's fine. It seems we've reviewed and confirmed all the major points.

Gao: Yes. And we'll have the final contract ready by tomorrow.

Notes:

[1] How long will this agreement be valid? 协议的有效期是多长？

[2] If this schedule ever changes, we will need a notice at least two months in advance. 如果发货时间有变化，需至少提前两个月告知我们。

[3] This provision has been duly noted in the contract. 该条款已在合同里明确指出。

[4] Could you walk us through the fine print? 你能给我们解释一下（契约 / 合同中的）附加条款吗？此处 walk through 可以理解为“逐步解释”，fine print 则表示（契约 / 合同中的）附加条款。

More to Learn for Dialogue 1

1. Main Clauses

(1) Can you tell me the main clauses in the contract?

(2) Shipment terms are essential to a contract too, aren't they?

(3) You must state the description of the goods, the quantity and the unit price in each contract.

(4) This provision/clause has not been included anywhere in the contract.

2. Signing the Contract

(1) We'll have the contract ready by tomorrow.

(2) It's time for us to sign the contract.

(3) Shall we sign the contract now?

(4) This is our contract in duplicate. Would you please countersign here?

(5) Our company signed the sales contract in the meeting room at 9 a.m. yesterday.

3. Coming into force

(1) The contract takes effect today.

(2) The contract in duplicate will come into force upon signature.

(3) This contract will be effective after being signed by both parties.

Dialogue 2

(Fu Qing, a sales manager of Beijing Import & Export Co. Ltd, is going to amend some terms and sign a contract with Mr. Ronald, a delegate from Alfred Co. Ltd, New York.)

Amending the Contract

Fu: Well, Mr. Ronald, here is the draft of our contract. Please take a look to see if everything is in order.

Ronald: Thank you, Mr. Fu. (Reading the contract.) Please excuse me for a while for checking all terms. [1]

Fu: No problem. (15 minutes later.)

Ronald: I think we've agreed on deferred payment for some of the items, but it has not been included anywhere in the contract.

Fu: I'm sorry for that. Let's write it into the contract then.

Ronald: OK. Also, I think we should add a sentence here like this, "If one side fails to observe the contract, the other side is entitled to cancel it, and the loss should be borne by the side breaching the contract[2]."

Fu: Oh, that's an important clause. I shouldn't have ignored it. Is there anything else you've noticed?

Ronald: Just one more thing. As you know, our order is usually in large quantities, and it takes at least 3 months for production. To ensure a timely delivery, would you please allow partial shipment and put "Partial Shipment Allowed" into the contract?

Fu: That's reasonable. We can amend it as requested.

Ronald: It seems we have agreed on all the terms and conditions now. Shall we sign the contract tomorrow?

Fu: Sure! We'll get the contract ready by 9 a.m. tomorrow. I'll see you at the meeting room of our company.

Signing the Contract

Fu: We've been looking forward to this moment, Mr. Ronald. Shall we sign the contract now?

Ronald: Of course.

Fu: Here are four copies of the contract. Please sign your name here. I'll sign here. (Signing the contract.)

Ronald: Done. Congratulations. (Shaking hands.)

Fu: Please keep these two copies, and we'll keep those two.

Ronald: Thank you. I'm looking forward to our continuing cooperation.

Fu: So am I.

Notes:

[1] Please excuse me for a while for checking all terms. 请让我花些时间检查条款。

[2] If one side fails to observe the contract, the other side is entitled to cancel it, and the loss should be borne by the side breaching the contract. 如果一方未能遵守合同，另一方有权取消合同，由此产生的损失由违约方承担。

More to Learn for Dialogue 2

1. Abiding by the contract

(1) As a buyer, we fulfill our contractual obligations under the contract.

(2) Both parties should abide by the contract.

(3) Our principles are to abide by the contract and keep good faith.

(4) We sincerely promise that both quality and quantity are in conformity with the contract stipulations.

2. Breaching the contract

(1) Any deviation from the contract will be unfavorable.

(2) It's clearly a breach of contract.

(3) You have no grounds for backing out of the contract.

(4) You have breached the contract and all subsequent actions will be invalid.

3. Canceling the contract

(1) Now we have no choice but to cancel this contract.

(2) The buyer has the right to call the deal off and cancel the contract.

(3) We would like to cancel the contract due to your delay in delivery.

(4) If one side fails to observe the contract, the other side is entitled to cancel it, and the loss shall be borne by the side breaching the contract.

Practice

Practice One: Matching

Match the sentences in the left column with the correct responses in the right column. Each sentence has only one response.

A. Shall we sign the contract now?	1. Of course not! You have a good reputation in this business. We believe that you can carry out the terms of the contract.
B. Let me propose a toast to the success of our negotiations. Cheers!	2. Yes, we will. But please inform us in advance about the available shipment.
C. You have had a busy schedule these days, haven't you?	3. This afternoon, and we will sign the contract at our office at around 4 p.m.
D. What do you think of the delivery terms?	4. Sure. Pass the pen to me, please.
E. Do you worry about the non-execution of the contract and non-payment on our part?	5. Well, I think that's all for it.

F. But in case there is no direct steamer, will you consider allowing transshipment? G. Now all the stipulations above are confirmed. Is there anything to add? H. When will the contract be ready?	6. Here's to our future cooperation. Cheers! 7. That is just what we need, and I am satisfied with that. 8. Yes, I have done a lot of things and visited several places.

A. ________ B. ________ C. ________ D. ________

E. ________ F. ________ G. ________ H. ________

Practice Two: Blank Filling

Fill in each blank in English based on the Chinese meaning.

(1) Shall we ____________________ to see ____________________?
（我们逐项检查各个条款，以确认我们完全达成一致，如何？）

(2) If there ____________________, we hope we'll ____________________.
（如果产生争议，我希望我们通过友好协商解决。）

(3) We'll see if ____________________?
（看看我们能不能再谈谈？）

(4) We can assure you that ____________________.
（我们可以向您保证我们会信守诺言，按合同办事。）

(5) Is it possible that ____________________?
（合同上这几个地方的文字描述可不可以这样改一下？）

(6) I want to thank you for ____________________.
（我想感谢您为这次交易所做的一切努力。）

Situational Practice: Creative Tasks

(1) Liu Jie, the General Manager of Zhejiang Silk Co. Ltd., is meeting Joe White from India. Joe White is the head of the Import Department of the Textiles Corporation. Liu Jie is reviewing the main clauses with Joe White. In the conversation, they should:

- greet the client at the conference room,
- confirm the details of shipment and payment,
- add one missing term to the contract.

(2) Chen Ping, a sales manager of Wells Import and Export Co. Ltd, meets a client, Miss Rose Black, in the conference room to modify the packing method and write it into the contract. In the conversation, they should:

- explain the reason for modifying packing,
- mention the relevant cost and difficulty,
- confirm the conditions of contract cancellation,
- decide when and where to sign the contract.

(3) Matthew Zhang, a salesperson of a Chinese Canned Fruits Company, just concluded a deal with an Australian company. They need to review the quantity, packing, insurance and time of shipment. Afterwards, a contract should be signed in duplicate. Make a conversation based on the details below.

Quantity: 500 cartons.

Packing: in cartons of 20 cans each.

Insurance: to be effected by sellers for 110% of the invoice value against All Risks.

Time of shipment: September 20, from Xiamen, China to Melbourne, Australia.

Knowledge Zone

I. How to Properly Sign a Contract So it Will Be Enforceable?

You've negotiated an important agreement, and reduced it to a written contract, now you are ready to sign on the dotted line. Most people think that actually signing a contract is a mere formality. However, it is important not to let your guard down at this point. Whether you properly sign the contract may make the difference between a smooth business transaction or a messy court fight.

The following steps should be followed when signing any contract.

1. Make sure the contract you're signing is the contract you agreed to sign

If the contract has gone through a number of rounds of negotiations or revisions, don't just assume that the copy put in front of you to sign is what you think it is. Before you sign it, be absolutely sure that you fully know and understand the terms of the document. You are generally bound by a contract that you sign even if you have no knowledge of its contents. Unless you can prove that the other party engaged in fraud or other wrongdoing in preparing the contract or inducing you to sign it, you will be required to abide by it.

2. Date the contract

Dating a contract will help you to positively identify it later if you need to and will help you place it in its proper chronological context. The term of a contract begins on the contract's effective date. Unless you state otherwise in the contract, the effective date is ordinarily the execution date — the date the contract is signed.

3. Make sure both parties sign the contract

This may seem basic (and it is!) but you'd be surprised at how often this slips one's mind in the hustle and bustle of getting on with business. Although you don't necessarily have to sign an agreement for it to be valid, why would you want to take that chance? There is absolutely no better way of proving that a party intended to be bound by a contract then by whipping it out and displaying their signatures on the document. If it is possible that the parties to a contract will not sign it at the same time, you might consider adding a section in the contract providing that the contract will not be legally binding unless it is signed by both parties.

The parties do not necessarily have to sign the same copy of the contract in order for it to be binding. If the parties do sign different copies of the contract, they must agree that their signature pages together constitute a complete executed agreement. That's why contracts often contain a provision stating that "the parties may execute this contract in counterparts, each of which is deemed an original and all of which constitute only one agreement."

4. Make sure any last-minute changes to the contract are initialed

The best course of action is to have any changes included in the signature version of the contract. This will help ensure there is no misunderstanding as to what the parties intended to sign. However, if it is not possible to have a contract revised and reprinted before it is signed, make sure that any changes made to the contract by hand are initialed by each party to the contract.

5. The parties must sign the contract in their correct capacity

If an entity is a party to a contract, it is imperative that the signature block properly identifies the party signing on behalf of that entity. For example, if someone is signing as president of a corporation, the signature block should look something like this.

Acme Widgets, Inc.

By:______________________

John Doe

Its: President

Why is this so important? Because signing correctly on behalf of an entity will prevent any later claims that the person signing the contract is personally liable for the entity's contractual obligations.

6. Make sure the other party has authority to sign the contract

The importance of this cannot be overemphasized. Obviously, you do not want a company to claim that it doesn't have to abide by the contract because it was signed by someone who was not authorized to do so. Thus, if the other party to the contract is a corporation, you need to be sure that the corporation is actually in existence, that the person signing on behalf of the corporation has the authority to do so, and, that the contract was approved by the corporation's shareholders or directors.

7. Keep an original signed copy of the contract in your files

Each party should get an original signed copy of the contract for their files. That means if there are two parties to the contract, two identical contracts must be signed. One original copy of the contract should go to you, and one original copy should go to the other party.

II. Five Common Contract Mistakes to Avoid

When drafting an important contract, it is easy to make mistakes. Business contracts can often be long and contain unfamiliar terminology. Attention to detail and a depth of understanding about what the parties to the contract are trying to accomplish are essential. A misplaced word, letter, or even punctuation mark can make a big difference.

Here are 5 common contract mistakes that you should avoid making.

1. Leaving It Unsaid

One of the worst mistakes that you can make in a contract is assuming that something is understood. Anything that you have agreed to but not addressed in a contract is probably not legally enforceable. A good habit to adopt is to ask yourself "Would this be clear if it was read by an arbitrator or judge who has no familiarity with the parties or the relationship?" If the answer is no, don't leave it unsaid — add objective clarifying language.

2. Using Vague Language

Besides the fact you typically get what you pay for when it comes to contract drafting, there is almost zero chance that the document or language you found will apply to your unique situation. Your contract should be created to specifically cover your own business. Using vague or ambiguous language can result in serious consequences, since it will not make sense if there is ever a need to enforce it.

3. Not Negotiating It

Preparing a contract is not the first step of a business transaction. Before a deal is memorialized in a contract, the parties must first negotiate the key terms. The next step is capturing the details and tying up any loose ends. Only then are you ready to choose the right contract structure for your deal.

For business relationships, the first contract you receive is often understood as an initial draft. If there is something you are unhappy with, negotiate it before you sign the contract! Make sure any additional changes are captured in writing in future drafts.

4. Ignoring an Endgame

At the start of a business deal, usually everyone loves everyone. Sadly, even the best working relationships sometimes reach a difficult end. Make sure your contract has clear plans for what the end goal of the relationship is, and what the exit paths are along the way. You should also include clear instructions on how to end the relationship prior to hitting your goal if need be.

5. Not Doing Scheduled Reviews

Once your contract has been signed, it is tempting to file it away and never look at it again. Sometimes that works out OK. More often, however, the relationship with the other party to the contract takes unexpected twists and turns. Frequently the best negotiated terms that made perfect sense when you signed the contract aren't fair or even applicable anymore a year or two into the contract's term. Schedule a contract review on your calendar (usually annual reviews are fine) just to sit down and make sure the provisions in your contract still reflect the real-life agreement between the parties.

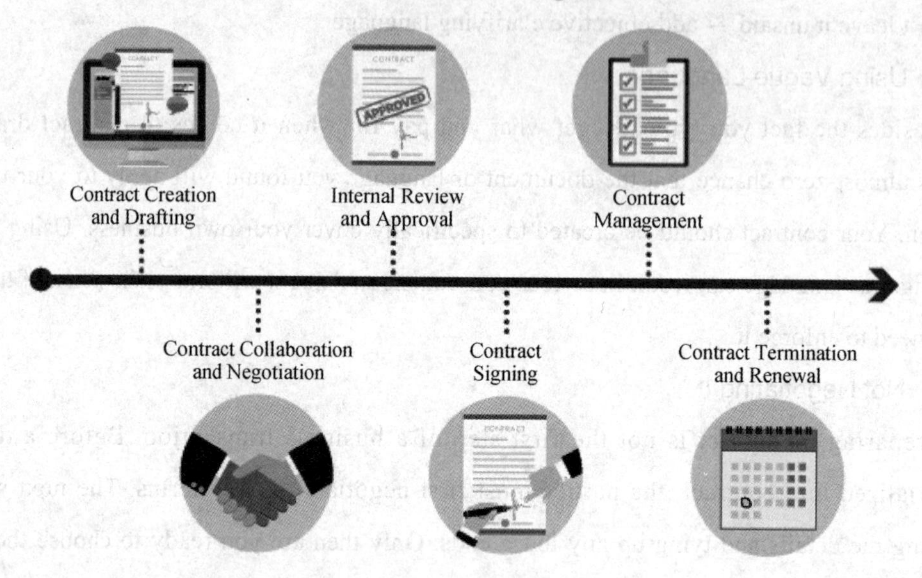
Guidance on Contract Management Timeline
Contract Creation and Drafting
Internal Review and Approval
Contract Management
Contract Collaboration and Negotiation
Contract Signing
Contract Termination and Renewal
CONTRACT
APPROVED

Unit 12
Settling Claims

Learning Objectives

- Lodge a claim as customer.
- Know the steps to settle a claim.
- Learn the skills of soothing customers.
- Keep good relations with customers after a claim.
- Master the basic expressions of settling claims.

Warm-up Activities

Task 1

◆ Brainstorming:

What will you do if there are some problems with the goods received from your supplier abroad?

Expressions of Claims

英文术语	中文翻译	英文术语	中文翻译
lodge/file/make/register a claim	提出索赔	claimee	被索赔人
entertain/accommodate a claim	接受索赔	claimant	索赔人
withdraw a claim	撤销索赔	claim statement	索赔清单
waive a claim	放弃索赔	claim letter	索赔书
settle a claim	解决索赔	claim report	索赔报告

Task 2

◆ Discussion:

How will you respond to an angry customer who files a claim against you?

Task 3

◆ Group Presentation:

If a foreign buyer files a claim against you for the wrong goods, how will you deal with the claim? Think it over and present it to the class.

Vocabulary

specification [ˌspesɪfɪ'keɪʃn] *n.* 规格，规范

compel [kəm'pel] *v.* 迫使；不得不

lodge [lɒdʒ] *v.* 正式提出（声名等）; *n.* 乡间小屋，门房

supervise ['suːpəvaɪz] *v.* 监督

transit ['trænzɪt] *n.* 运输，运送

compensate ['kɒmpenseɪt] *v.* 赔偿，补偿

defective [dɪ'fektɪv] *adj.* 有缺陷的；有瑕疵的

entrust [ɪn'trʌst] *v.* 委托，交托

incident ['ɪnsɪdənt] *n.* 事件

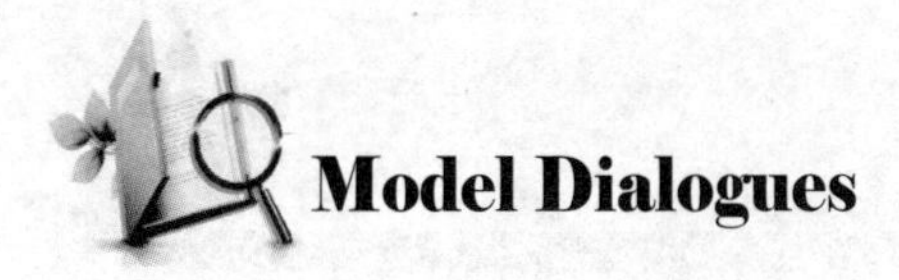

Model Dialogues

Dialogue 1

(Mr. Black is a representative of American Belling Import Company. He is calling Wang Lei, a salesperson from Shentai Trading company, to make a claim.)

Wang: Mr. Black, what can I do for you?

Black: Mr. Wang, we regret to inform you that the toys you shipped to us do not accord with the required specifications in the contract, and we are compelled to lodge a claim against you [1].

Wang: Can you explain to me exactly what the matter is?

Black: After the arrival of the goods, we are surprised to find that some of them are seriously damaged. This is the certificate issued by the security department.

Wang: I'm sorry to hear that. Our packing is always very strong, and suitable for long distance transportation. I think that this may be caused by careless handling.

Black: I'm afraid not. After the arrival of the goods, I supervised there almost every day. And the certificate also clearly tells that the goods are damaged in transit[2] due to the improper packing.

Wang: I'm really sorry. There must be some mistakes with the dispatch department.

Black: I think so.

Wang: I'm sorry for bringing you so much inconvenience[3]. I will give you a reply as soon as possible after checking the details.

Black: All right. I hope to receive your reply soon. Bye.

Wang: Thank you for your understanding. Bye.

Notes:

[1] We are compelled to lodge a claim against you. 我们不得不向您提出索赔。lodge a claim 意为“提出索赔”；也可以使用 file/make a claim 表达提出索赔的含义。

[2] in transit 运输中

[3] I'm sorry for bringing you so much inconvenience. 很抱歉给您带来这么多不便。

More to Learn for Dialogue 1

1. Lodge a claim

(1) I'm afraid we have to lodge a claim against you for the wrong color.

(2) We have to lodge a claim against you for the quality of the goods you shipped us on the 25th of June.

(3) We have to lodge a claim against you due to your failure to deliver in time.

(4) We have lodged a claim for short weight against the insurance company for USD 2,000.

2. Ask for the details — seller

(1) — Have you found the cause of breakage?

— Obviously, it was due to careless packing.

(2) — We haven't had any complaint of this kind. Is there any evidence?

— Certainly. Here is a survey report issued by the local inspection authority.

(3) — Could you tell us some particulars of it?

— We entrusted the local inspection authority with the task of reexamining the goods. The result of the inspection indicates that the damage was caused by poor packing.

3. Look into the problem — seller

(1) I'm sorry and I will check that immediately.

(2) I will ask our manufacturers to look into the matter.

(3) We need to check those damaged goods first.

(4) A careful inspection must be conducted first before drawing any conclusion.

Dialogue 2

(Wang Lei is a salesman of Shentai Trading Company. He is calling Mr. Black, a representative of American Belling Import Company, to talk about the settlement of his claim.)

Wang: Good morning, Mr. Black. I'm calling to talk with you about the claim you made yesterday. We've looked into your claim. [1] We have to admit that unqualified packing is one of the main reasons.

Black: You mean that you accept our claim?

Wang: Yes, in view of our friendly business relationships, we are prepared to accommodate your claim for the damaged goods. We'll replace any damaged items free of charge.

Black: That's nice. How about the extra shipping charges?

Wang: It is our fault, so we will pay the extra shipping charges.

Black: That is great. I do hope you will take care of your packing next time.

Wang: You can rest assured[2] that we will take every step necessary to ensure that no similar incident will occur again.

Notes:

[1] We've looked into your claim. 我方已就贵方的投诉开展了调查。

[2] rest assured 放心

More to Learn for Dialogue 2

1. Settle the problem — seller

(1) I understand how you feel. I will give you a reply as soon as possible after checking the details.

(2) If we find that's our mistake, we'll deliver new goods for compensation as soon as possible.

(3) I can see how you might feel that way. How about giving you a 5% discount for the wrong color?

(4) As for the shortage, we'll make that up quickly and we'll deliver that the day after tomorrow.

2. Reject a claim

(1) We are not in a position to entertain your claim since it hasn't been rechecked.

(2) We regret our inability to accommodate your claim without sufficient evidence.

(3) We can not entertain your claim. Your claim should be referred to the insurance company.

(4) We are not responsible for any damage that happened during transit. You may expect the shipping company to entertain your claim.

(5) As your complaint does not conform with the result of our test, please conduct another examination to show if there are grounds for your claim.

3. Entertain a claim

(1) In view of our friendly business relations, we are prepared to meet your claim for the 35 tons' short weight.

(2) We regret the loss you have suffered and agree to pay you USD 1,000 in compensation.

(3) We are prepared to make you reasonable compensation but not the amount you claimed.

(4) We'll contact our insurance company and pay for the damage.

(5) Our cheque for USD 5,000 was airmailed to you today in settlement of your claim for short weight of 1,000 tons.

Practice

Practice One: Matching

Match the sentences in the left column with the correct responses in the right column. Each sentence has only one response.

A. I ordered 10,000 pairs of women's shoes, but I received the same amount of men's unexpectedly.	1. We'll try our best to make sure that we ship the goods by the end of the month.
B. How long should we wait for? I hope our clients can get them before the New Year's Day.	2. I'm awfully sorry, sir. I was informed just now that someone in our company has made a mistake in filling your order.
C. How about the wrong goods?	3. That's great. I hope the same mistake won't happen again.
D. Can you do anything about the goods mistakenly shipped?	4. We are not responsible for any damage that happened during transit. You may expect the shipping company to entertain your claim.
E. The factory agreed to compensate for your damage.	5. We'll manage to send you the correct goods as quickly as possible.
F. I am sorry and we are responsible for the mistake. We will replace the goods that fall short of our sample.	6. The leakage of juice was brought about by damaged tins. They were evidently broken through careless handling while being loaded into the ship's hold at the dock in Sydney.
G. Whom should we claim with, the insurance company or the shipping company?	7. If you could sell them at the spot price at your end, it would be better.
H. Have your people in London discovered what were the exact causes of the leakage?	8. Thanks. I would like to know the details about the plan of compensation.

A. ________ B. ________ C. ________ D. ________

E. ________ F. ________ G. ________ H. ________

Practice Two: Blank Filling

Fill in each blank in English based on the Chinese meaning.

(1) Please give our claim your ______________________________.

（请合理考虑我们的索赔要求。）

(2) Please examine the matter and ____________________ as soon as possible.

（请调查此事，并尽快将货物发给我们以弥补数量的不足。）

(3) As regards ____________________, we claim ____________________.

（关于你方产品的品质低劣问题，我方要求你方赔偿一万美元。）

(4) We shall __________ incurred as a consequence of your failure to __________.

（由于你方未能及时交货，我方将就由此遭受的全部损失向你方提出索赔。）

(5) We regret that ______________________________.

（很遗憾，我们无法接受你方关于货物短装的索赔。）

(6) We hope this ______________________________.

（我们希望这一不幸事件将不会影响到我们双方之间的关系。）

Situational Practice: Creative Tasks

(1) Shirley, a representative of Sunshine company, calls Lily, a salesperson in HB Import and Export Company, to lodge a claim for the short weight/wrong color/damaged goods/inferior goods/poor packing/delayed delivery. The talk should include the following points:

- description of a claim,
- apology to the client,
- promise to a settlement.

(2) Lily, a salesperson in HB Import and Export Company, calls Shirley, a representative of Sunshine company, to tell her the settlement of her claim (short weight/wrong color/damaged goods/inferior goods/poor packing/delayed delivery). The talk should include the following points:

- purpose of calling,
- settlement of a claim,
- negotiation of the settlement.

(3) Your client is very angry about the delayed delivery which leads to his failure in

catching the selling season. He lodged a claim against you and you should carefully deal with his claim and make every effort to retain him.

Knowledge Zone

I. How to Deal with Customer Complaints

Part 1 Addressing the Complaint

1. Take a deep breath and put your emotions aside

When someone is complaining about your business, it can feel like an attack. But you need to remain as calm and emotion-free as possible to help successfully deal with the complaint.

2. Introduce yourself

When you meet the customer or she picks up the phone from your call, be sure to introduce yourself in a friendly manner. This can help reassure the customer that an actual person is there to listen to her complaint.

3. Listen to your customer's entire complaint

Listen to her until she finishes to show that you are taking the complaint sincerely and seriously.

4. Apologize and sympathize

Apologize to and sympathize with her to show that you understand how she's feeling.

5. Restate the complaint and ask questions

Restate her complaint and ask questions to help you better understand the situation.

6. Thank and reassure your customer

Make sure to thank your customer for her thoughts and answering your questions. Offer her reassurance that you're going to address the complaint in a timely manner and find a solution.

7. Confirm follow-up details

Make a plan with the customer to follow up her complaint. This can help reassure her and remind you to take care of the complaint quickly.

Part 2 Following Up with Your Customer's Complaint

1. Investigate the complaint

Before you find a constructive solution to your customer's complaint, investigate the situation further based on her description of events.

2. Formulate an acceptable solution

Come up with a solution to the complaint that works for everyone. Consider having alternatives in the event that a superior or the customer doesn't agree with it.

3. Contact the customer

Call or write your customer with the solution you have for her complaint.

4. Offer your solution

Kindly offer the solution to her. Remember to keep your tone warm and sincere so that she knows you genuinely care about her complaint and the solution.

5. Thank her again

Our customer may be feeling a little embarrassed that she created a fuss. Thank her again for her concern and tell her you're available if she needs further assistance.

6. Learn and move on

Even though the situation may have initially been negative, you can use it as a learning experience. Take the process of addressing and following up the complaint as a constructive way to handle future complaints. Don't dwell on it, either, because most businesses will receive occasional complaints, some of which have nothing to do with you or your work.

7. Engage with your customer again

After some time has passed, consider contacting your customer to make sure the resolution was satisfactory. This can show her that you value her business and allows you to address any potential problems.

II. Resolution of Disputes in International Trade

It is very important to arrange contracts properly in international trade. In commercial relations, even if the parties make every effort and act meticulously to fulfill their commitments, it is inevitable that disputes will arise due to various reasons. These reasons may arise from the faults of the parties, as well as outside the control of the parties, such as customs procedures, labor laws and practices, translation errors or deficiencies. Although it is essential to resolve the problems between the parties, it is possible to resolve them with outside assistance. In order to resolve disputes quickly and cost-effectively, some solutions are suggested. These solutions are as follows:

1. Negotiation

Negotiation is the least formal of the ways to resolve disputes. The negotiation method is a voluntary method, and it may also have some legal consequences. Negotiations are carried out when the parties decide to resolve the dispute themselves. Although it is not mandatory to have a lawyer or representative in negotiations, it is very useful to have them.

2. Mediation

The most common amicable resolution of disputes is mediation. Unlike negotiation, mediation uses a neutral third party to assist the parties in reaching an agreement. The purpose of mediation is to reach an agreement that the parties can mutually agree to. The mediator agreed by the parties should first explain the procedure to be followed, emphasizing that he/she is an impartial person. Then, he/she should get information from the parties, determine the issues that form the basis of the dispute, listen to the parties and ask questions, observe them and discuss the solution options with the parties and encourage them to come to an agreement. If the negotiations are successful, the mediator should assist the parties in drafting the agreement that will resolve the dispute. A properly prepared agreement will have resolved the dispute, as it can be enforced when necessary. In addition, notary publics participating in the documentation process can be used as mediators in the resolution of disputes. The independent and impartial position of notaries will enable them to gain the trust of the parties, if they are appointed as mediators, so that dispute resolution negotiations will take place in a more moderate and productive environment.

3. Arbitration

Arbitration is the most common solution method used for disputes in international commercial transactions. Arbitration is the agreement between the two parties who have fallen into dispute, leaving the resolution of this dispute to private individuals, and the dispute being examined and resolved by these persons. These special persons, whose resolution of the dispute is left to them, are called "arbitrators". Arbitrators have no official capacity to resolve the dispute submitted to them. However, by transferring the resolution of the dispute to them, the parties consent to the decision of the arbitrators. In this way, the arbitrators become a court in terms of the case they are dealing with. For this reason, arbitration is also called an "arbitral tribunal". If the parties consider resorting to arbitration in international commercial disputes, they must first choose one of the two ways of arbitration. These are ad hoc arbitration or institutional arbitration.

4. Litigation

The most familiar type of dispute resolution, civil litigation typically involves a defendant facing off against a plaintiff before either a judge or a judge and jury. The judge or the jury is responsible for weighing the evidence and making a ruling. The information conveyed in hearings and trials usually enters, and stays on the public record. Lawyers typically dominate litigation, which often ends in a settlement agreement during the pretrial period of discovery and preparation.

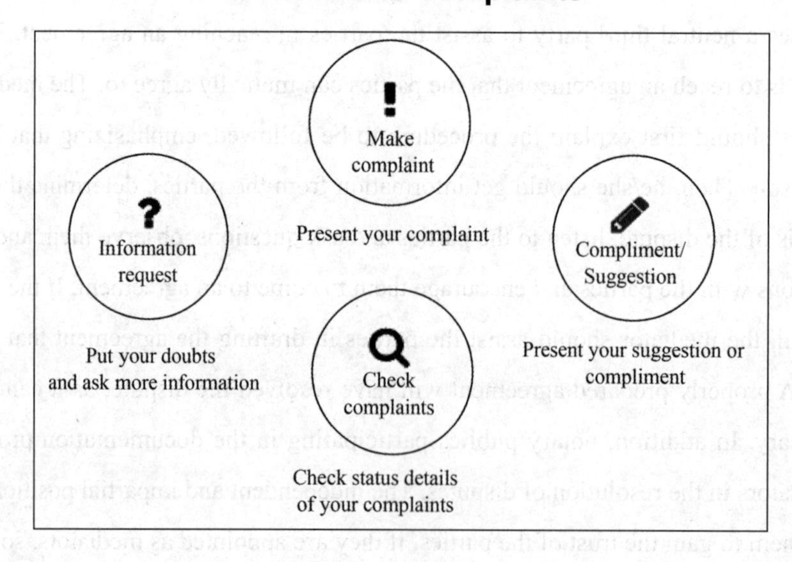

常用外贸术语缩写

A

AR: All Risks 一切险

AWB: airway bill 空运提单

ATTN: attention 某人需留意

A/C NO.: account number 账号

ASAP, a.s.a.p.=as soon as possible 尽快

B

B/L: bill of lading 提单

Bal.: balance 余数

B.D.: bank draft 银行汇票

b.e., B/E = bill of exchange 汇票

bill discounted: 贴现票据

B/G: bonded goods 保税货物

bg. ; b/s: bag(s) 袋

br.: brand 商标；牌

bxs.: boxes 箱（复数），盒（复数）

C

CFR: cost and freight 即 C&F，成本加运费价

CIF: cost, insurance and freight 成本保险加运费，也称“到岸价”

CPT: Carriage Paid To 运费付至目的地

CIP: Carriage and Insurance Paid To 运费、保险费付至目的地

CIC: China Insurance Clause 中国保险条款

COD: cash on delivery/collect on delivery 货到付款

CY: container yard 集装箱堆场

CY-CY: 场到场（集装箱堆场到集装箱堆场），用于整柜的装箱方式

CFS: container freight station 集装箱货运站

CFS/CFS: 站到站（货运站到货运站），用于拼箱货的装箱方式

C/D: customs declaration 报关单

C.C: Collect 运费到付

CNTR NO. : container number 柜号

CTN/CTNS: carton/cartons 纸箱

C/(CNEE): consignee 收货人

CO; C/O: certificate of origin 产地证

CHB: customs house broker 报关行

COMM: commodity 商品

CTNR: container 集装箱

ca.; c/s; cs.: case or cases 箱

ct = crate 板条箱

C.A.D.; C/D: cash against documents 付款交单

C.B.D.: cash before delivery 先付款后交单

Cert. ; Certif.: certificate; certified 证明书；证明

cgo.: cargo 货物

chges.: charges 费用

Chq.: cheque 支票

credit: 贷方；信用证

cu.cm.= cubic centimeter 立方厘米

cu. in.= cubic inch 立方英寸

cu. m.= cubic meter 立方米

cu. yd. = cubic yard 立方码

D

DDU: delivery duty unpaid 未完税交货

DDP: delivery duty prepaid 完税交货

DEQ: delivered ex quay 目的港码头交货

D/D: demand draft 即期汇票

D/P: document against payment 付款交单

DOC: document 文件、单据

Doc#: document number 文件号码

D/A: document against acceptance 承兑交单

doz./dz.: dozen 一打

D/O: delivery order 发货单

DOC: direct operating cost 直接操作费

dstn.: destination 目的地（港）

E

EXW: ex work/ex factory 工厂交货

ETA: estimated time of arrival 到港日

ETD: estimated time of delivery 开船日

ETC: estimated time of closing 截关日

EXP: export 出口

EA: each 每个，各

encl(s): enclosure 附件

encd: enclosed 附件

End., or end: endorsement 背书

F

FC: free carrier 货交承运人

FAS: free along side 船边交货

FOB: free on board 船上交货（也称“离岸价”）

FCL: full container load 整柜

FAC: facsimile 传真

Form A: 产地证（贸易公司）

F/F: freight forwarder 货运代理

FOC: free of charges 免费

F.O.: free out 船方不负责卸货费用

F.I.: free in 船方不负责装货费用

F/L: freight list 运费单，运价表

f: feet 英尺

G

G.A.: general average 共同海损

gal.: gallon 加仑

G.W.: gross weight 毛重

gr.: gross 罗

grm.: gram 克

gsm: gram per square meter 克每平方米（丝绸计量单位）

GSP: generalized system of preferences 普惠制

GSP C/O: generalized system of preferences certificate of origin 普惠制产地证

GSP Form A: generalized system of preferences Form A 普惠制格式 A

H

HB/L: HOUSE BILL OF LADING（货代提单）

H/C: handling charge 代理费

hrs.: hours 钟点

I

ICC: International Chamber of Commerce 国际商会

ICC: Institute Cargo Clause 伦敦保险学会条款

Inc.: Incorporated 有限公司

Incl.: inclusive 包括在内

Inst.: instant 即期

INT: international 国际的

INV: invoice 发票

IMP: import 进口

I/S: inside sales 内销售

K

kg: kilogram 千克

kilo: kilometer 千米

kv: kilovolt 千伏

kw: kilowatt 千瓦

L

L/C: letter of credit 信用证

l.: liter 公升

LG: letter of guarantee 保函

Ltd.: limited 有限公司

M

MB/L: master bill of loading 主提单

MIN: minimum 最小的，最低限度

MAX: maximum 最大的，最大限度

M or MED: medium 中等，中级的

m: meter; mile; million 米；英里；百万

M.O.Q: Minimum Order Quantity 最小订单量

N

NVOCC: Non Vessel Operating Common Carrier 无船承运人

N.W.: net weight 净重

N/F: Notify 通知人

n.: net 净值

O

OA: open account 赊账 / 销

OD: overdraft 透支

OEM: original equipment manufacturer 原始设备制造商；贴牌生产；代工

O/F: Ocean Freight 海运费

OB/L: ocean bill of lading 海运提单

O.G.: ordinary goods 中等品

OP: operation 操作

ord.: ordinary 普通的

o/s: out of stock 无现货

P

POD: port of destination 卸货港

POL: port of loading 装运港

REF: reference 参考、查价

RMB: renminbi 人民币

P.A. : particular average 单独海损

P/A: payment on arrival 货到付款

pd: paid 已付

POR: payable on receipt 货到付款

PR 或 PRC: price 价格

P/P: freight preraid 运费预付

P.P: prepaid 预付

PKG: package 包，捆，扎，件等

PC/PCS: piece/pieces 只、个、支等

P/L: packing list 装箱单、明细表

PCT: percent 百分比

PUR: purchase 购买、购货

Q

QA: quality assurance 质量保证

QTY: quantity 数量

qr.: quarter 四分之一；一刻钟

R

R&D: research and development 研究和开发

Re.: reply 回复

RSVP: reply, if you please 请回复

S

S/M: shipping marks 唛头

S/O: shipping order 订舱单

SEAL NO.: seal number 铅封号

S/C: sales contract 销售确认书

S.S: steamship 船运

S/(Shpr): shipper 发货人

S/R: selling rate 卖价

T

t.b.d.: to be determined 待决定

T.C.: traveler's check 旅行支票

thro., thru: through 经由，通过

tks: thanks 致谢，感谢

tkt: ticket 票

Tr. : transfer 转让

T/T: telegraphic transfer 电汇

T/S: transship 转船，转运

U

UCP: Uniform Customs and Practice for Documentary Credits 跟单信用证统一惯例

ult.: ultimo 上月的

U/T: unlimited transshipment 无限制转船

U/M: under-mentioned 下述

V

v: refer to 参见

V: volt 伏

vs: versus 对

via: through, by way of 经由，通过

VOCC: Vessel Operating Common Carrier 船公司

W

W. A.: with average 水渍险；单独海损要赔险

WB, W.B.: waybill 运单

wf: wharf 码头

wk: week 星期

W/T: weight ton 重量吨（即货物收费以重量计费）

WTO: World Trade Organization 世界贸易组织

W (with): 具有

w/o (without): 没有

W/R: warehouse receipt 仓单

X

XL: extra large 特大

xs.: excess 超过

参考文献

[1] 沈银珍 . 外贸英语口语（一）[M]. 北京：中国人民大学出版社，2014.

[2] 沈银珍 . 外贸英语口语（二）[M]. 北京：中国人民大学出版社，2014.

[3] 江海波，董亮 . 外贸英语口语 [M]. 杭州：浙江大学出版社，2010.

[4] 沈婵，方志仁 . 外贸英语口语 [M]. 北京：中国石化出版社，2011.

[5] 王慧，仲颖 . 外贸英语谈判实战 [M]. 北京：中国海关出版社，2016.

[6] 丁俏蕾 . 外贸英语口语实训教程 [M]. 北京：清华大学出版社，2014.

[7] 李科科 . 老外最想与你聊的 100 英语话题 [M]. 北京：中国宇航出版社，2012.

[8] 张莹安 . 旅游英语口语入门 [M]. 北京：外语教学与研究出版社，2018.

[9] 郑仰霖 . 观光旅游英语通 [M]. 南京：江苏科学技术出版社，2015.

[10] 李雪，李铁红，范宏博 . 旅游英语口语大全 [M]. 北京：机械工业出版社，2014.

[11] 金利 . 终极酒店英语话题王 [M]. 上海：华东理工大学出版社，2016.

[12] 朱华 . 酒店英语视听说教程 [M]. 北京：高等教育出版社，2014.

[13] 公晨，陈芳 . 酒店英语口语 [M]. 武汉：武汉大学出版社，2016.

[14] 范广丽，袁立辉 . 餐饮英语教程：上册 [M]. 北京：对外经济贸易大学出版社，2010.

[15]（美）费内坎普，张苹 . 餐饮英语口语一本通 [M]. 北京：旅游教育出版社，2016.

[16] 戴卫平，张丽丽 . 外贸英语话题王 [M]. 北京：中国宇航出版社，2011.

[17] 刘新法 . 外贸英语口语一本通 [M]. 北京：中国海关出版社，2008.

[18] 李雪，李铁红，范宏博 . 外贸英语口语大全 [M]. 北京：机械工业出版社，2014.

[19] 廖瑛 . 新编外贸英语口语教程 [M]. 3 版 . 北京：对外经贸大学出版社，2014.

[20] 郑敏 . 外贸英语对话 [M]. 北京：中国财富出版社，2018.

[21] 杨国俊，邱革加，黄滨 . 实用外贸英语阅读 [M]. 武汉：华中科技大学出版社，2004.

[22] 罗虹，陆志兴 . 国际经贸英语阅读 [M]. 武汉：武汉大学出版社，2007.